Having a Pen of a Ready Writer

Virginia Freelon

www.WeAreAPS.com

Copyright © 2019 Virginia Freelon

All rights reserved.

No portion of this book may be reproduced mechanically, electronically, or by any other means, including photocopying, without written permission of the publisher.

ISBN: 978-1-945145-06-3

Table of Contents

Acknowledgements

Introduction 1

Chapter One: What's On Your Mind? 4

Chapter Two: Having A Prison Mindset 8

Chapter Three: God Is Speaking To Your Circumstances 22

Chapter Four: A Way Of Escape 28

Chapter Five: A Brand New Day 43

Chapter Six: Being Outside of Your Comfort Zone 63

Chapter Seven: Go Collect Your Goods 70

Chapter Eight: Release Your Glory 81

Chapter Nine: My Testimony 98

Chapter Ten: Breakthrough Prayers 119

Acknowledgements

When you find yourself reading this book, you will be able to tell what's been on my mind and what I've been thinking lately. Mostly, I've been thinking about you. During this separation, I found it was not easy being apart from you. I missed all of you when I had to excuse myself from all of my family, friends and loves ones. I was enduring hardship like a good solider. Thank you for your patience and understanding. Thank you for not giving up on me. With heartfelt gratitude of love and with tears of joy in my eyes, I acknowledge all of you and I am entirely grateful to God for my time well spent with Him during my absence from you.

#SigningOff: With Tears of Joy....

Introduction

Everywhere you turn in life you will encounter a divine intervention. You may say to yourself, "I should or could write a book or journal, or even start a blog". Surely, you have pondered over several of these options to begin writing something – even if it just a business plan. Many times you may have found yourself grabbing a pen and paper and probably having bits and pieces of notes everywhere and just haven't put them together yet. You've said to yourself, "I wonder if I should; I'm going to do it this time". If you constantly say, "One day", then my answer to you is, "Just do it". Go ahead and start with your introduction. From there, write out your first chapter, and don't stop until you reach the end of your storyline.

As I began to ponder in thought, I found myself writing until the break of day. As I continued writing, I heard, "Write the vision and make it plain" (Habakkuk 2:2). As I kept writing, I saw a stage, and I was standing there, the curtain was drawn back. I began to speak what I was writing. The words were flowing through my pen. It was like a big eraser board in front of me and I had to write out and say what I was writing one hundred times over and over again:

I CAN ACHIEVE WHAT I BELIEVE
I CAN ACHIEVE WHAT I BELIEVE
I CAN ACHIEVE WHAT I BELIEVE

It was a type of punishment assignment, you know, like when you were in grammar school. It was the beginning of achievement gain and accomplishing the ability to overcome the fear of becoming an author.

My pen kept writing, and I asked, "God, what am I going to write about?" Suddenly, I felt like writing and telling my whole life story. I just started jotting down all my thoughts that kept running through my mind. I felt like crying it out on paper. I felt like writing a storybook type of novel. I felt like singing a melody and writing it on paper. From there on, I started writing and speaking miniature sermons of, *Having a Pen of a Ready Writer*. My journey into my next book became history. "I can achieve what I believe" became alive. I overcame my fears and accomplished my goal. I am an author. I achieved one of my greatest accomplishments when I wrote my first book, *Singles Ministry with a Vision and Purpose.*

I encourage you not to stop writing; keep writing. Every writer starts with a thought, a divine intervention, life experience, song, sermon or writing out your prayers. Enjoy the journey of reading a group of miniature sermons and the effectual fervent prayers of a righteousness man that availeth much. Praying on the behalf of others is leading me into my third novel, *To God Be the Glory*.

Be prepared to have a ready pen and paper near your bedside and write down what's on your mind. Every divine thought that springs forth in your mind will appear in different levels and seasons, and not always in sequential order. You might be sleeping and have to wake up in the middle of the night. You might be driving and have to pull over, or take a break while at work and walk away from the task at hand. Whatever the case, be ye ever ready to write your next speaking engagement, sermon, or song.

Having a Pen of a Ready Writer can lead you into your next novel. Psalm 45:1 says, "My heart is inditing a good matter: I speak of the things which I may have made touching the king: my tongue is the pen of a ready writer." Our first and last thoughts of our days and nights should be in prayer. Remember, "I can achieve what I believe" so that you can.

Thank you in advance. Have a blessed and prosperous journey into writing your next novel. Enjoy!

CHAPTER ONE

What's on Your Mind?

Be ye ever ready to preach or teach what thus saith the Lord.

Have a sermon written upon your heart, in your pocket, somewhere. Just be prepared with a ready pen and paper.

The timing of a spoken word will appear in seasons. Sudden revelations will start pouring forth one after the other. Have I done my first sermon? No. It all happened for me after my second workshop and a couple of open conferences. I started writing and expressing what God was saying to me.

I asked, "God, what are your people thinking, and what's really going on in their minds? Do they truly have the mind of Christ? Are they really hearing from you? Are they listening to your voice, or the voice of others? Who are the other voices they're listening to – the governor,? the President,? the mayor,? Priests,? or Kings? You said that your sheep hear your voice and another they will not follow."

As I continue to obey the voice of God, I hear other voices. They are the past sheep without a shepherd. So, I ask, Which one are you? Be ye ever ready to hear the voice of God's calling. His direction is very clear.

Rumbling Noise

In the spirit realm, there is a rumbling of a loud thunderous movement and a mighty rushing wind that is swirling through this city. It appears like a huge chess board and many people are standing around being moved in different positions. The kings men and the pawns are not in their rightful places. The people of God are being scattered all around with indecisive minds. I know they are waiting to hear the same message spoken over and over, year in and year out. "You are going to get a bigger house. You are going to drive a Bentley. Money is coming to you now".

The rumbling is so loud to those that have an ear to hear and receive. "My word will not return unto me void" said the Lord. "For I have given you to inspire men in the past and I am now using inspire men today to speak a sure word or a prophecy of my word over their lives like never before. And it shall come to pass."

The thunderous sound that you are hearing right now is not the message that I have prepared. There are some missing pieces on the chessboard that are not connecting together. If you have ever played chess before, you know there's a lot of concentration; you cannot make any sudden moves. You must plan ahead and make the right move so you won't get blocked or pushed back. You have to strategize your move and you can't make it too soon.

Turn around and tell somebody. Don't make your move too soon.

These loud thunderous sounds can make you jump or be fearful. They can have you move prematurely – make you move when you should be standing in your position. Be still and be quiet before you make the WRONG move. The wrong move will take you out of your position and move you to another church, which is not a bad move if God placed you there.

A pawn on a chessboard can only be moved diagonally. It can't be moved all over the place; it has to be put in position. I learned to play chess at an early age by my father, and I critiqued it from my first husband (my daughter's father). Pawns can only be moved one square at a time. They are considered foot soldiers marching forward or going in a different direction as ordered.

You have other pieces on the board – the rook and knight. They work unanimously left to right. Let's not remain focused on the chessboard as we look at the leadership in churches or the White House cabinet.

CHAPTER TWO

Having A Prison Mindset

Having a prison mindset is not just being in jail cell or being locked up behind four walls; it's about being locked up behind your thoughts. There are people that can contain your thoughts through mind-controlling spirits. Anyone that has control of your whereabouts, what you can say, who you can see, is an influencer known as a controller. A controller is a person that operates out of witchcraft and is known as a witch or warlock's spirit.

A witch or warlock spirit tries to control your mind to manipulate you into doing things outside of your character and tries to take charge of your thoughts. When you're unaware of their subtle devices they will use clever indirect methods to achieve and captivate your thinking patterns by controlling what you're thinking and how you're thinking. They will even try a more subtle approach to convince you that you're delusional.

Just like the devil who goes about seeking whom he can devour. You can become preoccupied wondering about looking for your parking space, trying to find your glasses or where you placed your car keys. 1 Peter 5:8, "because your adversary the devil, as a roaring lion, walketh about, seeking whom he may devour." One he can confuse you into thinking that something is wrong with your normal way of thinking.

Satan's job is to keep you from claiming the mind of Christ. Because he knows that God has given you a sound mind to function out of the peace of God that surpassed all of your fears. The purpose of witchcraft is to wear you down little by little to control your life. Its purpose is to keep you entrapped behind your own will and emotion always wrestling with unbelief and doubt, which bears a spirit of uncomforted feelings of uneasiness.

Beware of Jezebel spirits that function through people, places and things. These demon spirits of Jezebel work to get you to blame others for your own actions because you're feeling a certain way. Never recognizing your own wrong doings or those minor things of misplacing something, not completing a goal or a project you've been working on for months and years. Using excuses such as, having a minor headache; not getting much sleep; overexerted. Living in and out of forgiveness and all other malfunctioning problems and concerns that keep you bound as you continue to blame others for your own actions.

A Jezebel spirit releases a witchcraft spirit against your mind, will and emotions so that you can't see a way out of a certain situation. A Jezebel spirit carries other spirits such as lust and enticements, alluring you into different types of behavior by controlling your actions. Remember, these are your thoughts that have you trapped behind the four walls in your mind. The very moment you realize you have been caught up in a snare, you must seek counselling and find a way of an escape from your own thought patterns without blaming others.

This spirit that you have allowed yourself to be entrapped by is called a prison mindset. It has been created by your own negative thoughts along with other people that you have allowed to influence your thinking. All negative thoughts form an imagination of everything around you. It keeps you from staying focused and having a clear vision towards your goals.

Have you ever wondered how you got entangled with being locked up inside the walls of your mind, but you can see yourself on the outside of the cell looking in? In order to see yourself free from that prison controlling thought would be to reconnect with your inner spirit that dwells from inside of you. Once you realize what has captured you from the inside of these four walls of that prison jail cell, you will begin to fight and help find your way out. "The violent take it by force" to overcome every trap that is set before them.

When you tune into the process of your thoughts and the way you've been thinking, you will begin to see yourself free from the issues of what have been keeping you bound and locked up. This statement is a profound one and once you grasp it, you will hear it with a ringing sound: "Whom the son sets free is free indeed." It has a sound that states "in thee" in Christ, our Lord, our Savior who sets us free in him, who delivers us from all doubts and fears when we cast all our cares upon him. The word *indeed* confirms our freedom; it releases us from an unwavering spirit. It opens the door to exit out of what we have conjunctured in our lives throughout our generation. *Indeed*, breaks the curse of bondage.

Just looking at the definition of *indeed*: it is used to emphasize a statement or response confirming something already suggested. "It was not expected to last long, and indeed it took less than three weeks" Synonyms: as expected, to be sure, in fact, in point, of fact, as a matter of fact, in truth, truly, actually, really, in reality, as it happens/happened, certainly, surely, for sure, undeniably, veritably, nay, if truth be told, you could say: archaizing, sooth, verily "there was, indeed, quite a furor" yes, certainly, assuredly, emphatically, absolutely, exactly, precisely, of course, definitely, quite, positively, naturally, without (a) doubt, without question, unquestionably, undoubtedly, doubtlessly, indubitably; by all means; informal, you bet, you got it, I'll say "are you well? Indeed!" 2. Used to introduce a further and stronger or more surprising point: "The idea is attractive to many men and indeed to many women."

I probably didn't need to address them all but, this word alone by all means has captivated all kinds of people, places and things. All doubts and indecisive ways of unbelief, everything that God states we are free from. The first thing that came to my mind was to start by looking at your surroundings, who you've been seen talking to; what's in front of you; and what you need to do to get out of the situation that has been holding you back. What put you in that position? Who came and bewitched you and made you think you was what they said about you? Learn how the spirit of witchcraft operates and how it will play mind games with you by trying to lock you into their ways of thinking, which now have become a lie.

And we know Satan is the father of lies that goes about roaring like a lion seeking who he can devour. He was a liar in the beginning according to John 8:44-47, "You belong to your father, the devil, and you want to carry out your father's desires. He was a murderer from the beginning, not holding to the truth, for there is not truth in him. When he lies, he speaks his native language, for he is a liar and the father of lies. Yet because I tell the truth, you do not believe me? Can any of you prove me guilty of sin? If I am telling the truth, why don't you believe me? Whoever belongs to God hears what God says. The reason you do not hear is because you do not belong to God." Anything which functions outside the will of God belongs to the devil. Beware of the tactics of the spirits of witchcraft.

Thoughts that are mind controlling spirits that will keep you locked up and tied down into the way of believing what they say, how they do things, go where they tell you to go all because they are afraid of losing you. They begin saying negative things like, "If you leave, you're not going to grow, you're just going to sit down and not be used". They talk against your purpose, goals and destiny toward your future. When you encounter these types of manipulating spirits and begin to hear people talking in that manner, you should walk away.

The many voices in your head will tell you if you don't follow their rules and plans for your life you will never become nothing and you're going to remain captive to their thought's patterns.

When you don't seek God and follow the Holy Spirit, they can take advantage of your weakness. When you release yourself from that prison mindset of their way of thinking and cast all your cares over to God, you will see yourself free from all your issues. "For whom the son set free is free indeed."

Don't play by their rules; they are setup to keep you locked in a jail cell that was created by man to keep you from fulfilling your destiny. Don't just move when they move or when they say move. You would think that's how you're supposed to live – under the direction of another man's thoughts, rules and regulations.

Everybody needs a guide that is functioning out of the spirit realm of the Holy Spirit, not through spiritual wickedness and spirits of witchcraft. Know the fruit of the spirit; try the spirit to see if it is of God. The enemy comes in to steal, kill, and destroy; otherwise, he has no reason to send a spirit of distraction to the people of God. He comes into your house, your church, your spirit to strongly attack you because he's after your purpose. He's breaking in to steal your goals. He's out to kill your peace and joy, which are your ammunition along with your strength. When he finds you weak, he brings seven other spirits to entrap you from furthering your purpose.

He's breaking in to destroy your family, your marriage, your children, grandchildren, and your relationship with Christ.

However, God came to set the captives free that you may live and not die. He will give you the authority to overcome all the power of the wicked spirits that came to override you. As long as you keep your mind in the presence of God, you will overcome the thoughts that try to captivate your mind.

Although the attack appears strong, you have a shield of protection surrounding you from every assault from the enemy. No weapon formed against you shall prosper as long as you stay in the presence of God, which is your safety zone. You are able to walk upon scorpions and serpent that will help you to triumph over all the works of every evil device that come to weaken you from reaching your destiny.

In life our faith will be tested. One thing for certain and two things for sure; there are angels of light surrounding us day and night watching to keep us from all harm and danger that may keep us from conquering and pursuing our goals. Rest assured, we have been given angels to charge over us daily to guide us into new open portals. They provide a way of escape from every obstacle that tries the spirit by the spirit that weaken our faith that is formed against our mind. Stand firm in the authority placed inside of you so those things that you are striving toward shall come to pass.

The declaration that was once made still exist and is standing strong. "I would never leave you nor forsake you"; "My words will not return unto me void"; "Hold fast to my words. If, I said it, I will perform it and it will be established. Speak the word of God over your life and set yourself free from behind your prison cells you created through your imaginative thoughts. Start confessing,

"I will", obtain greater in this season and every trap the enemy set will be defeated; every spell that has been cast against me by the sorcerer's, witchcraft and naysayers will be destroyed and cast down by the Holy Ghost.

Every witch and warlock spirit, every divination spirit will return back unto their sender. These types of spirits are formed in different types of shapes – triangles, octagons, squares, and diamonds – not easy to recognize. Their works of darkness will be defeated. For I decree and declare over our lives that we are more than conquerors against all the works of the spirits of wickedness. Through the power of the Holy Ghost that has been invested in us through the Holy Spirit.

The spirit of Jezebel is known as a woman, but that spirit is used as an example to define the spiritual works of the wicked one. A jezebel spirit is know as a controller a person that operates out of witchcraft spirit that controls your mind, will and emotions so that you can't see any way out of your situation. It also carry on other spirits such as lust and enticements that allure you into all different types of behavior.

Every experience that you have encounter in your life God has giving you the power to overcome every controlling manipulator, influencer, and spiritual wickedness in high places. Power to destroy the very works of their plots and plans they've created behind these prison jail cells through the captivity of your mind.

Once you overcome what capture you inside of these four walls of that prison jail cell you will begin to fight and find your way out. "The violence takes it by force."

Imagine being captured in your prison mind on the battlefield as a marine scout sniper. The only choice you have is to take out every enemy in your path to get to your next designated point. Remember, these are traps set up by your opponents that have been created by your thoughts and visions. You're no longer locked up behind these cells of your mind that had you bound inside these four walls looking in not recognizing your freedom. You are about to escape what your mind has been telling you. You are free to open up new portal gates in your mind by speaking to your situation and confirming you are no longer locked up. Right there you begin to run as far away from that prison cell. You stopped to take a deep breath and look back. There is nothing there so you turn around and now darkness has come upon you and there's nowhere to turn. You're praying for one second and now you're standing in the enemy camp in the middle of a battlefield. People are running, screaming, shouting; guns are being fired and grenades being thrown. You are standing with a rifle in your hand and you are aiming to fire at that one person that have you bound. Now you've become a sniper, what are you going to do?

The first thing you must do is regain focus. As a sniper, you have to have a clear view in spite of everything that is going on around you in order to keep a clear vision towards your next move. You must keep your mind clear of your surroundings for your next purpose, which is completing your goal.

God is the center of your purpose. He has designed a clear and purposeful life for you. Our God given purpose is to remain steadfast, unmovable always abounding in the things that are essential around Him. Staying focused on our purpose helps us gain total balance concerning our family, our priorities in life. By surrendering our total concerns towards God regarding every issue that involves our entire being.

Exodus 9:16, "But I have raised you up for this very purpose that I might show you my power and that my name might be proclaimed and all the earth." Having the power of the Holy Ghost and in the power of the name of Jesus, you will keep your mind free from any mindset that come to imprison you. Once you surrender your will over to God to fulfill his purpose in your life, your purpose will be fulfilled. You will no longer be locked up in your mind. You will begin to fulfill the plans and thoughts you set out to accomplish. They will come to pass and will work together for your good. Proverbs 19:2 says, "Many are the plans in a person's heart but it is the Lord's purpose that prevails and every plan that you have set out to make."

First, you must start with having the mind of Chriist in order to break free from any attack of the enemy. Seek God for His direction and ask, "What must I do to get free from behind these prison walls in my mind?" Stay in the presence of God daily and dwell in the secret place of the most high. Repeat the 91st Psalms, "I shall dwell under the shadow of the almighty". This will help encourage you from every obstacle that is set before you and free your mind from bondage so that you can have the mind of Christ. Having the mind of Christ there is liberty and whom the son sets free will remain free from all bondage of mindsets in Jesus' name. Amen.

Awareness of Your Freedom

Here's a brief summary that just ruffles my feathers every time I hear about all the crime going on. We got *black lives matter, white lives matter, lesbianism and homosexuality lives matters.* American lives matter, yet we are still fighting against one another, killing one another, backbiting and gossiping against one another. We just really need to get it together regardless of race, color or sexual preference.

Homosexual, heterosexual whatever you find yourself in at this particular moment of your life, time is winding up. If you don't know by now, God is not returning with fire or a flood, but He is surely going to return in a twinkling of an eye. One of the main sins that will keep you out of Heaven is backbiting and gossiping.

Repent, and turn from your evil ways and thoughts.

Another thing that ruffles my feathers is to hear of two women fighting over some "sorry tail man" or some men fighting over some "sorry tail woman" (don't ask me why I use this word "sorry tail," I heard it from somewhere.) These types of relationships ends up in violence over he said/she said stuff that ends up in murder, broken relationships. It's just terrible. The majority of time it's about a man sleeping with another woman or woman sleeping with another man. Why fight one another this type of behavior when you can just walk away, instead b of being put behind bars or living in bondage?

Relationships should be committed in a convenant agreement teaming up together to help each other to grow and better understand one another. Women should come together and get the one that is cheating on them both instead of fighting one another. If either person cared about the other, they wouldn't end up in this kind of situation.

The man should be God-fearing, put God first, and seek His face to have the woman God has ordained for his life in marriage. If this happened, the aforementioned behavior would not be taking place.

The woman of God will have confidence to trust God that He would not place her in this kind of position because God has ordained them to live a godly and pleasing life before Him knowing that God is able to supply the proper spouse to be in their lives, even if there is dating before they get married.

Pray that he or she will be the person that loves you and only you without the drama. Pray that he or she wouldn't put any other man or woman before you that will be a uncomfortable position for the both of you. And, know that God is speaking to that situation of infidelity in both of your lives. God is still speaking to your situation through awareness. God warns his people in advance he states in 2nd Chronicles 7:14, "If my people who are called by my name will humble themselves and pray turn from their evil ways, then will I hear from heaven and heal the land and every situation you may be wrestling with. This includes your relationships, your marriages and your household.

That's God's way of constantly giving us a way out of our relational situation, financial situation. God is constantly pointing us in a different direction, but we refuse to obey and seek His face.

The Lord says, "I'm constantly opening up new doors for you to walk into and you choose to pick door number three." A man's way seemeth right before his own eyes with pride and before pride comes destruction before his fall. Be aware, stay alert, watch and pray. Because the adversary is roaming about seeking whom he may devour.

CHAPTER THREE

God Is Speaking To Your Circumstances

With a loud voice as when he cried out to Lazarus to come forth in John 11:43 (KJV), "And when he thus had spoken, he cried with a loud voice, Lazarus, come forth."

Whatever circumstance you're wrestling with, God is calling it by its name: marijuana, cancer, diabetes, lung disease, sexual perversion, homosexuality, just to name a few; it must flee in Jesus' name. It will come forth and you will come out of that situation that has you bound. Speak to that situation that has you weighted down with the cares of this world. Speak to what is keeping you wrapped up in a dead clothing. Untie yourself and began to shout out, "I am free from the bondage of sin. The sins that I've been carrying around they no longer have me bound."

Whether, it's about a man, woman, finances or a job. Whatever you're going through, God will deliver and set you free from it when you pray to Him. Even if it didn't happen, speak to it with a loud voice. It shall come to pass as it is stated in Deuteronomy

28:1-14, "I shall not die but live and declare the works of the Lord", and so it is. In Psalms 118:17, "My deliverance, my breakthroughs are happening today God promise it and so shall it be established."

As you continue to confess and submit that problem before the Lord and speak to it with your voice, it should fully come to pass.

Every problem, situation or circumstance you're entangled with in this very hour. As of this day, speak to it and say with me, "Whom the son has set free is free indeed" John 8:36. Say to that circumstance, "I am delivered from that. I am released from every situation that had me entangled with the yoke of bondage. I no longer live in my flesh; I am now walking in the newness of my life." Take time out to read Roman 7 at your leisure. Read the entire chapter every day and watch your life change before your very eyes.

That circumstance, situation or problem that once had you trapped, tied up or down as of today God is speaking to it on your behalf and commanding it to come forth and come out from amongst you. You must tell it to flee. Your newness has now become that light in darkness that had you caught up in a snare. By speaking to it and calling it out, you are no longer bound. That sin has now been broken off your life and you are free to live a sinfree life. Walk in your authority and power to live a life of Freedom.

Speak to sickness and say, "I am healed".

Speak to poverty and say, "My God will supply all my need".

Speak to your attitude and say, "I am redeemed".

Walk out of those graveclothes. You are delivered and made whole to live a free filled life. Free to live in the spirit of God; you are no longer bound to that situation, circumstance or problem any longer. God is speaking with a still small voice on your behalf.

Start looking at your situation as a bud, a flower that's growing into something as the most beautiful thing you ever seen in your life. Then that circumstance that once held you back will began to blossom into the fullness, the new flower you have become. But you must be the one to water it with the word of God daily, so find time out from your daily routine and surroundings of your peers to read a scripture that relates to your growth. Start to relate to what's really been on your mind and what you have been thinking lately without being weighted down with everybody else's thoughts.

Examine yourself by starting your day reading a scripture or two. Try Philippians 4:19, "But my God will supply every need". All of your resources are going to come from Him. Trust God to provide for you everything you need in your day. Seek Him out daily. Remind Him of His word. Remind God what He said about you. Practice talking to God.

Your second reading of scripture will be III John 3:2, where he says, "Beloved, I wish above all things that you should prosper and be in health even as your soul prospers". These are the words that will begin to shift and transform you into your destiny and change your entire atmosphere to flowing and moving you back into the kingdom of God.

Don't be Alarmed

You will begin establishing your power to reign over every opposing demonic force that tries to come and keep you from moving out of that circumstance or situation that had you bound. Start praying: where there are two or three touch and agree with the confession of their mouths the words of life will begin to bring down every stronghold and every work of the devil. Call those things forth as though they were and you will have the victory over every one of them that tries to cause the defeat in your life. God said it in His word and it is so. Everything He created was good and you should eat the good of the land.

Supernatural explosions are taking place right now to conquer and release the power of God's love, joy, and peace in the Holy Ghost. God's word says with His stripes you are healed from every bondage and anything that is not releasing His healing power is being cast down and destroyed. God spoke with authority and said, "Satan, the Lord thy God rebuke you."

God has given us dominion over all unclean spirits to speak

against all soul diseases and every situation to pull it down. We cast out every problem and say, "You have to go". No temptation has come to overtake us there is a way of escape.

The devil is going around like a roaring lion seeking who he can devour. So be sober and vigilant and be aware not shaken. 1Peter 5:8.

For at this very hour you need not fight in this battle; this battle is not yours to fight. What God has promised it shall come to pass, stand still and see the salvation of the LORD. He is going to work this together for your good. Be ye ever ready. Stay alert. Continue to fast and pray, for prayer is the key that will unlock the mystery.

Don't be alarmed. The mystery that will soon be unfolded and will bring new insight to new life in your new beginning. These are just a few things that I have in store for you. 1 Corinthians 10:13, "God is faithful and he would not let you be tempted beyond what you can bear when you are tempted, he will also give you the ability to endure temptation as a way of escape."

Having the Heart of God

God will give you a heart to be on one accord and to know your pure purpose concerning your situation. He will continue to give us a heart to stay focused on purpose of prayer that we may hit the mark on the areas in which we are called to pray. We pray on behalf tonight for the people of God in this world system. We thank you in advance for your power that is going to move even on this day.

Every intercessor from the north, east, west and south has been summoned to break up the fallow ground of unrighteous living, for this is the heart of God. We pray on behalf of each family member that is in our midst to shift and be transformed into a different level. We know God has shifted and changed our position and His heart is pure. Thank you for every exaltation of your prayers, God, and we thank you in advance. Thank you for moving like never before in Jesus' name.

CHAPTER FOUR

A Way of Escape

There are two doors in front of you - an exit and entrance door. The question here would be, how are you going to choose your exit and your entrance at the same time? First, you must come to a conclusion that there is no temptation formed against you that will be able to keep you from entering your exit or exiting your entrance. Remember God is faithful and He will forever provide a safety zone for your way of escape.

1 Corinthians 10:13, "No temptation has overtaken you that is not common to man. God is faithful, and he will not let you be tempted beyond your ability, but with the temptation he will also provide the way of escape, that you may be able to endure it."

Be prepared to do the necessary work for your next level that is going to lead you through the doors that are before you. One way or another and two things for sure, you must choose. Your exit is going to be your entrance that is going to help launch you into your future plans. Your entrance is going to be your exit that is going to help bring you out from amongst anything that tries to prevent you from your destiny.

Every day, every week, every month and every year ahead of you is opening up a greater opportunity for you to receive your breakthrough. There is nothing standing between you and your decision, but you. The only thing that is preventing you from going forward is you having a halt between two opinions. Your thoughts and your decision of choosing the right door.

It's going to get better. Look around and see yourself improving and seeing the hands of God upon your life creating witty ideas for you to move forward into your next level. Your way of thinking about things are not the same; your thinking pattern has been redeveloped. The things that used to distract you don't bother you or matter as much anymore because you have a different mindset.

You see yourself choosing more of the exit doors coming out of a situation or circumstance that had you locked up from entering into your destiny from the beginning. Your approach to life is much different when your outlook on situations and circumstances no longer have control of your rightful decision making skills.

You've learned how to handle things differently.

Remember, some things come into our lives to teach us a lesson, and some things we must learn how to walk away and close the door behind us. Walk away from it, let it go and let God handle the situation no matter if it's a person, habit or addiction.

Whatever it is that is blocking your way of escape into your next level, your destiny or your future, "be careful or anxious for nothing but in everything pray about it, seek God about it and cast your cares on the Lord" Philippians 4:6. When you look around in the world and it seems like it's spinning out of control, check out your exit and entrance zones for way of escape.

God has given us a way of escape on purpose.

We are no longer bound by the world's chaos. Be not entangled with the yoke of bondage, for whom the Son sets free is free indeed. If the Son therefore shall make you free, He should make you free indeed. God has delivered us and will deliver us again. 2 Corinthians 1:10. Therefore, we are able to live in this life until eternity until Jesus returns. That's what He promised and we must stand firm on His promises and see the salvation of God move on our behalf.

Take up your positions.

Stand firm and see the deliverance that the Lord has given unto you. You'll see that "you will not need to fight in this battle." 2 Chronicles 20:17. Be not alarmed by the terror by night, I have provided an exit door for your way of escape. "Enter into my gates with thanksgiving and into my courts with praise. Be thankful unto me and bless my name for the Lord is good."

Psalms 145; is one of my escapes, "There is a master plan that I have in store for your success and your future". Follow the manuscript that is set before you.

Turn the pages for your next exit, it will be your entrance into your next dimension. It's not to your left nor to the right but God is getting ready to blow your mind. God is going to blow your mind as you exit out of one door and enter into the other door of your entrance. It's right in front of you. It's always been there for your protection.

I have provided another plan for you, to prosper you and give you an expected end for your next level.

All you have to do is enter into your new dimension. Run with it and don't look back. Once you enter the entrance door you have chosen, you have a choice to stay or exit; you cannot keep running in the front door and exiting out the back door. You must make up your mind, and the only way you can do that is with the mind of Christ. That way, you already will have made up your mind that you're going to stay.

You'll be able to stick it out to the end with your first plan for the degrees and dimensions to your next level of success. In order to complete this, you must have the mind of Christ and put Him first in all that you plan to do concerning your life's successes.

Everything ahead of you depends on which door of opportunity you are going to choose; whom you will serve? Will it be God or man? Whether, you go into business for yourself or continue to work for someone else, you must choose. But remember, God has always provided a way of escape.

For it is written, "All things is working together for our good" Romans 8:28. Things will turn around again; keep making an about face.

God Will Make A Way of Escape…Part II

1 Corinthians 10:13, "There have no temptation taken you but such as is common to man but God is faithful who will not suffer you to be tempted above that you are able but will with the temptation also make a way of escape that ye may be able to bear it."

Some may say, no temptation, but God says, "with the temptation, he will also make a way for your escape." Some may say, "so that you may be able to bear it." Despite the cares of the world, there is always a way of escape. There will always be an exit door for your entrance into your next level.

The levels of faith have shifted into another dimension from faith to faith and from glory to glory. Your entrance door is your exit door, and your exit is now your entrance into your future. This next level of escape is your endurance to keep moving in the direction that has opened before you. Patience is going to be a requirement once you enter into this open door; you must wait patiently for the outcome concerning your new path. Don't get impatient and miss out on your supernatural breakthrough.

Seek ye first the kingdom of God to endure this hardship like a good soldier. Bearing all things and doing all things for God will give you a way of escape. By searching out the word hardship; which will be found in 2 Timothy 2:3-5; suffering as a good soldier of Christ Jesus. For no soldier gets entangled in civilian pursuits (worldly activities) since his aim is to please the One who enlisted him. An athlete is not crowned unless he competes according to the rules of the game. Another way of escape is bearing all things which will be found in 1 Corinthians 13;7: love bears all things, believes all things, hopes all things and endures all things.

As you begin to put all you have into believing every exit and entrance God has provided for you, whatever you're holding onto just open up one of those doors that you're standing in front of and let it go.

If it doesn't belong to you let it go.

T.D. Jakes may have put it this way "if anyone can walk away from you let them go." But, here's my take on that statement with new revelation and insight: Don't use that as a way out because the person walking away has a very legitimate reason to let go as well. If you don't belong to them, they have to let you go and walk away and they must let you go in order for each one of you to hear the voice of God and reach your next destination when He directs you to let go, let it go.

God brought you out of that thing that had you bound a long time ago and because you refused to; you end up staying too long in that situation you should have been let it go days, weeks, month or years ago. You should have been walked away but the different traps of mind-sets that came to hinder your growth from your ways of escapes that God had provided kept you from walking away.

For it is written and for it is also true; "whom the Son sets free is free indeed." When a person gets free, he's been set free to walk away from any dead situation that is not benefiting or profiting him in his growth or moving him into his or her divine purpose or destiny.

Whatever You're Holding on to, Let It Go….

Ask yourself this question: What am I holding on to that is keeping me from moving into my next destiny?

Whatever you're holding on to, it doesn't belong to you. God said, "I can only bless you with more when you let it go". If you have something or someone that doesn't belong to you, God wants to release it from your life today.

Some of us need to regain or change our name.

I was told a long time ago to change my name back to my father's last name, which is Young, and I still haven't done it yet. If I combine his whole name my father's name is "Plunder Surry Young" because I learned his side of the family is very wealthy. What I'm saying is his first name means to take it by force what rightfully belongs to him his goods, his inheritance just in his name alone. It represents value, goods and forcefulness.

And, I'm going to leave that right there.

There is a lot of inheritance in some of our forefathers' names. We can only reap the inheritance out of it when we let go of what we're holding on to. We only receive what has been sowed unto us when we let go of what doesn't belong to us. We should stop holding on to somebody else's name when God has delivered us from them. Even God has given us a name that is above all other names and some of us don't want to accept this God given name that has been freely given to us by His son, Jesus Christ. The one and only true and living God who died on the cross and bore all of our soul diseases.

Even when God set out to pray in John 17; He said, "All those that you have given me in your name are now mine". There's a lot affected in a name and when He sets out to pray that prayer, He was defining those that carried out His name sake in John 17:9-12,

"I pray for them. I pray not for the world, but for those whom you have given me for they are yours. All mine is yours, and yours are mine, and am glorified in them. And I am no longer in the world, but they are in the world, and I am coming to you. Holy Father, keep them in your name, which you have given me that they may be one, even as we are one. While I was with them, I kept them in your name, which you have given me. I have guarded them, and not one of them has been lost except the son of destruction that the scripture might be fulfilled."

What's in a Name

Even before a woman takes on another man's name; she has to be careful of what name she is attaching herself to as every name represents something or someone behind it. We can see the same way before we get married to a person. Right here is a place for us to minister to our younger women in our midst that are coming up in the body of Christ and in our ministry. A time to explain to them the importance of who they attach themselves to before marriage, before they give up their inheritance to the wrong hands.

This is not where I was going with this whole message but, when it got rerouted, I got excited.

Like Elizabeth did when Mary showed up at her door, once she experienced a visitation from the Holy Spirit, the baby leaped in her belly. So suddenly I felt another shifting that came concerning what's in a name, reminded me of this story about Elizabeth and Mary. That's when I felt compelled to start writing down what I've been thinking.

When this particular title or word came forth, I jumped up and grabbed my pen and paper with excitement and started writing what was going on in my mind and in my spirit man. At that very hour, I realized the importance of how we must be ever ready to hear what the spirit is saying to the church.

We often hear, "The church is in me so I don't have to go to church", but how much are you acknowledging what the spirit is saying to you and how often are you obeying the direction of the spirit? Even then you have to pick yourself up, follow the instructions given then be ever ready to hear the voice of God.

When you connect in the spirit, the main words that are spoken to you during your night season, during your meditation seasons or during the day is the very word of God, which is spoken through His still small voice, "Pick up your cross and follow me". Even if the church resides in you, you must pick it up and bring it into the temple, the sanctuary or the church.

It can't be explained any simpler than this.

Right at that very moment, a new revelation of sowing and reaping springs forth. A breakthrough of sowing into the kingdom of God is getting ready to hit the people of God in a much greater of understanding about sowing and reaping an harvest.. But, before I release the depth of that information. I need to share my testimony of what has been spoken to me. As you read on you, you can reach up and grab some and say, "I'll take some of that".

Whatsoever a man soweth that shall ye also reap Genesis 6:7-8. For it written; what a man soweth ye should also reap what ye have sown, that sounds very personal. What you've sown. You often hear if you not sowing anything, you're not going to reap the benefit from others who have sown because that strictly belongs to them.

Sowing can also be both good and evil according to the mindset of how you sow, what you sow and who you sowing into. If you sowing into something that is not producing any growth into your seed sown then you may not want to continue to sow into that. If you always find yourself saying, "There they go again asking for money" you just aborted your seed. Sowing with a cheerful spirit helps you to reap bountifully. So, if you're sowing with a good attitude on fertile ground, you will reap good soil. Planting good soil brings on good harvest. When you speak to your seed sown tell it to go, grow and return to me and that right soon.

Well, here I go again thinking about something entirely different than what I started out with.

The main subject line I came across in "What's in a name," and what caught my attention about this was the Rechabites who are the descendants of "Rehab", who were known as obedient children. They were used as an example by God to obey the instruction of their father. Jeremiah, the weeping prophet, who was sent to speak to the Rechabites and bring them to the house of the Lord, he was instructed to take them into one of the chambers and offer them wine to drink. Jeremiah 35:1-2.

People of God, there's never been a problem with wine; it's just God didn't drink it. He made it, but didn't drink it.

The problem is not with drinking wine, but with consumption of how much wine you drink that may take you out of character. It states in 1 Timothy 5:23; "to drink no longer water, but use a "little" wine for thy stomach sake and thine often infirmities. So, let's emphasize a little and to "heal thyself of some of your illnesses."

Now, the Rechabite's being taught to be obedient children were taught not to drink no wine neither them or their children after them. Jeremiah 30:5-7; "they rejected the offer from Jeremiah reminding him of their fathers' instructions." How many of us are willing to follow the instruction of God, who is known as our Father in heaven?

You have some church people that still think that it is okay to drink wine and have taken certain scriptures out of context to use it for their benefit. Such as, 1 Timothy 5:23 as stated above. What I'm getting at is you should think about who you are letting influence you from obeying the Holy Spirit. It's those that have received the gift of the Holy Spirit and have been born again with repentance who refuse to drink wine because Jesus didn't. In other words, as it is written; "obedience is better than sacrifice." I Samuel 15:22, or is it to "obey is better than sacrifice".

"I, beseech ye therefore, by the mercies of God that you present your body as a living sacrifice Holy and acceptable unto God, which is your reasonable service. And be not conformed to this world: but be ye transformed by the renewing of your mind that ye may prove what is that "good, and acceptable, and perfect, will of God." Romans 12:1-2.

As the Rechabites, we should not settle for anything that is outside the will of God holding on to the lust of our eyes or being easily persuaded by others who can entice or influence us into this disobedient spirit from obeying God's commandment.

Just a brief moment to relating back to that Jezebel spirit of influence.

In spite of the situation they were placed in, they did not yield over to their influencer, circumstances or temptation they were faced with or who were placed in front of them. They were able to stand their ground in time of adversity and remain obedient to their Father's instructions.

Keeping a Clear Vision

Help us to keep the instructions that are laid before us as we pray to the Father. Give us a clear tunnel vision for us to do the things you will have for us to see. Enlighten our eyes to see and hear our surroundings through Your eyes and ears. Let us hear Your voice. You said, "My sheep hear my voice and no other they will follow or hearken unto". Give us a clear word of Your righteous visions for our next season coming. Every year is the beginning of a new thing coming into existence.

Prepare our hearts to receive.

As of today, you can say, "No more being outside of the will of God, no more.

Nevertheless, not my will but thy will be done. Keep me Lord Jesus under the shadow of your will. Let me not be led by man's decisions and man's ways. If another man see himself free to drink wine let it be their desire, and if you desire Lord that I drink not of wine, let it also be with thee.

Protect our surroundings and give us clear vision that we might see the fulfillment of Your purpose and Your will concerning Your plans for our lives. That we may search out Your empowerment and Your plans that You have planned through

Your will for Your people which has been given to you by God your Father in Heaven and called by Your name.

CHAPTER FIVE

A Brand New Day

God, prepare us for a brand-new day. Thank you for a brand-new day where my circumstances have no power over my outcome; where my obstacles test my endurance in pleasing you by trying to strip me through my circumstances that are standing before me. As I continue to confess with my mouth, I will be victorious in my brand new day. I will be victorious over all of those who rise up against me.

As it is written in your word, so it shall be, I am no longer bound in my brand new day. I will seek the wisdom of God, for I need his guidance to move me into my next dimension; every breath I take into this brand new day. I will encourage myself to move forward and not be stagnanted, but develop me to improve my areas so I can step into a brighter tomorrow. The truth is, I should remind myself daily that God is what He says He is to me; God will do what He said He will do and He will keep what He promise unto me. I will succeed in everything in my brand new day that is put before me, that is put into my mind. I will start speaking God's word daily for all things that He has in store for me shall come to pass. I will not fret about anything any longer. I will just be grateful towards how God has been turning it around for my good.

Thank you once again for a brand new day where every circumstance against me has no power over my outcome. I won't be afraid of the terror by night nor the arrows that flieth by day. Or be alarmed by the devil that's going around like a roaring lion seeking whom he can devour. As it is written, "You need not to fight in this battle"; it is not yours to fight. I will repent of all my ungodly doings to be restored before God.

What God has promised He will do; He will turn it around for our good and it shall come to pass. Stand still and see the salvation of the Lord; He is working it together for our good. Stay alert and continue to fast and pray. For prayer is the key that will unlock the mystery to your future.

In my brand new day, I will see the wisdom of God for I need His guidance to move me into my next destiny.

Spiritual Nuggets: "Eye for an eye will only make the whole world go blind." Unknown Author. You will think but why did God inspire them to say an eye for an eye, and etc., you can study that at your leisure.

Wisdom is the Key

For wisdom is more moving than any motion she passes and going through all things by reasons of her pureness, for she is the breath of the power of God in a pure influence flowing from Glory of the almighty. Therefore, can no defiled thing fall into her to corrupt her. For she is the brightness of the everlasting light, the unspotted mirror of the power of God, and the image of His goodness.

For this is still the wisdom of Solomon. Proverb 8:11, For wisdom is better than rubies and all the things that may be desired are not to be compared to it". God grant me the courage not to give up what I think. Give me the wisdom and courage to stand in the greatness of my storms. Help my unbelief when I can't see the things You have before me and how to go about it to make it happen. You set the stage and vision of what my eyes and mind perceive.

Spiritual Nuggets: When we see the works of hell beginning to break loose and manifest. When we see human flesh failing miserably. God says we have the right to immediately step into that situation in prayer. Calling all intercessors to step in on its behalf. You have been given a role, which is to bring triumph of the cross of Jesus Christ to bear upon that situation. Unknown Author

During the process, I just meditate on his word for direction. As the spiritual nuggets pass through my mind.

TIME OF MEDITATION: "What a mighty God we serve. Angels bow before him. Heaven and earth adore him. What a mighty God we serve." This is all about having a pen as a ready writer, what have you been thinking lately and what's been on my mind starts to unravel once again. I just stop what I'm doing and begin to meditate in this very hour. Envision yourself awakening in love with a song down in your soul, rejoicing in your spirit, a praise in your feet, a clapping in your hands, and shouting in your voice declaring Victory is won.

Just to awaken in His presence allows you to come before His presence and thank Him because He is a mighty God that stands in the gap for all of our needs. Ever providing for us day after day. He said He'll never forsake us nor leave us. What a mighty God we serve. Always answering our prayers and when we think our prayers are going unanswered, if we wait, they shall come to pass. What a mighty God we serve. Angels bow before Him. Heaven and Earth adore him.

What a mighty God we serve.

God is forever opening doors for you, don't turn around to see who is following you just keep walking though the doors that are opening before you. There are multiple doors that are opening for you even on this day and you don't have to turn around to see who's following you or who's behind you just keep walking through the doors into your next destiny.

Continue to go forward forgetting those things which are behind you and pressing toward the mark of the high calling before you. Philippians 3:14

The new doors are being open towards you that the mighty God is opening for you. Everything you need at this hour is through the doors that God is opening, that no man can shut and no man can open. Isaiah 22:22, "The doors that God is opening in this hour no man can close."

Every prophetic spoken word that has been spoken over your life under the mighty word of God is coming to pass. God is speaking to you; will you set aside a time of intercession for such a time as this; to read a scripture daily?

Learn how to preach to yourself, prophesy over yourself, speak a word over your life, and "study to show yourself approved". 2nd Timothy 2:15. Because the voice activates that has been released is in your praise. It is in your song of worship. When you hear a song, sing it out loud with a shout.

God is waiting to hear from you.

If it's, What a mighty God we serve, the Angels bow before Him, just start singing because every knee must bow before Him. All men should bow before Him; all nations is going to bow before our King. The mayor will bow before our king, the government will bow before our King, education will bow before our King, the economy will bow before our King. Celebration will bow before our King, religion will bow before our King, families will bow before our King and the media will bow before our King. Intercessors throughout this nation has been praying for this very thing to come to pass for century and we have now come into agreement that it is so, In Jesus Name. Amen!

If angels bow before Him, we and everything present will have to bow before Him. Every woman, man, boy or girl must bow before the King of Kings and Lord of Lords. Habakkuk 2:11, "I will stand up on my watch and set me upon the tower and will watch to see what he will say unto me and I should answer when I am approved."

Remain in the place of position that He (God) has set before you.

Get in Position

Haggai's position was to imitate the act of reconstructing the temple, while Zechariah's position was to complete the work and get it ready for God's people for proper worship in the temple after its completion.

These are just a few storylines that is running through my mind as I grab my pen.

Haggai related to God's promised as a covenant, the consequent, commitments and dispensations. Haggai 2:23; says, "On that day declares the Lord and I will make you like a signet ring (he didn't say you are a signet ring already) for I have chosen you". Right here is where you ask God, what is a signet ring? You have been given authority to tread upon scorpions and serpents and every wicked and evil spirit that had you bound is now under your feet. As it has been stated, you have been chosen as one of God's own, known as His sons and daughters. Now declare your victory. Your time of meditation and consecration before the Lord starts now, you have been chosen get in your position.

I will be announcing the curse caused by the sin of Jacorachin and his descendants and symbolize God renewed covenant with his people securing the Davidic lineage of the Messiah.

Whose voice are you listening to? Be aware and stay alert.

Zachariah 7:9-10 expressed God's desires for social justice to administer justice is to show mercy and compassion towards one another. Zachariah's, vision confirmed the continuation of God's covenant with the Israelites.

Being in position to hear the voice of God may sound strange to others. Even when they read it, even when other ministers are being taught to position themselves to speak a word of life over the nation, over the people lives in there congregation. It may sound strange when they have spent this time alone with God and been in the presence of Him (God) to speak to live over certain circumstances and situations concerning the people of God and the Nations.

Then be ready to be open enough to share a word of life. To people who are not always ready to receive what God has given to the man or woman of God.

It's not always a good position to be in. You just have to forget what the people will say and get in your position and be ready to hear the voice of God. Hear what He is speaking to you concerning the homeless; those that are hungry; those that are sick; those that are jobless.

Just stay in position.

Spiritual Nugget: The Elite Squad is not sitting down watching others work.

Everybody's plans, purpose, destiny and lives are different. You have business people, church people, spiritual people and drunk people, yet everybody has been created in the image and likeness of God to be different from one another.

The selected elite squad is set up in the ministry for such a time as this. At your leisure, read Matthew 27:7, Luke 27:19 and 1 Corinthians 11:24.

Each act could be an act of improvement; does now begin tomorrow or does now begin today?

"The mind is a terrible thing to waste". Author Unknown

Our Days are Numbered

Psalm 90:12; "So teach us to number our days, that we may apply our hearts to wisdom."

Are we created to be in the same day? No.

God teaches us to number our days. Each day we live, we live out our divine days that have been created in the image and likeness of God who have created our days for His divine purpose. With every breath we breathe, we breathe a breath of life from this day.

There are appointments that are set up and there are appointed days, ordained by God. But, each day is scheduled differently from the other. We may have the same appointment but our purpose for that same appointment is different from another person's appointment. We may walk in the doctor's office at the same time but our appointments for that particular doctor will be fulfilled for the divine purpose that was set.

Our days are numbered.

The moment we open our eyes, we have entered into a brand new day. The very essence of that day depends solely on you, how you fulfill it and how you carry it out. Of course, it is written; "this is the day that the Lord has made and we should rejoice and be glad in it." It also has a lot to do with what is going on in that day for you. How many appointments you have fulfilled.

But, in this hour it's important that we stay on one accord in our days to come because we don't know how this day is going to end.

But, because we trust God to fulfill all our days, we pray that it ends well. Even as this day ends, we are living out this day together in this same hour, moment and at the same time. Functioning out of different capacities, and different locations and areas. We pray that we captivate the time in which that day will carry out in order to fulfill what this day brings forth. Just don't let this day pass you by.

As the first step in our day, we should seek out God's ordained plans for our brand new day. Planning our day on the instruction given to us by God. Don't get caught up being pulled in two directions.

Matthew spoke a word of truth when he said, "Seek ye first the kingdom of God". By seeking him of which way you should go, you will find all those things that is needed in your day. They will be in order for you to accomplish what you set your day out to fulfill when you allow God to guide your steps. As it says in Psalm, "The steps of a good man are ordered by the Lord."

When you allow God to guide you in your day, you're be set for one direction and, it will be marked in your calendar or posted for you to see it. When you see it, revelation will come forth and you will be guided into all truth that you will be moving in the right direction. Some decision in which way you should go is going to have be made by choosing which day you are going to be available and what day is going to take prevalence over the other day.

Our days are going to be numbered based on God's timing and seasons for our lives. Based on the days He has ordained and chosen for the rest of our lives. Matthew says, "We know not the day or hour He will come". Chapter 25 verse 13.

We may know the day and time the soap opera is coming on and based on each actor that is carrying out the scene for that day. Each of their performances is based on a decision of who should do it or what is going to take place in that particular scene on that day. The spirit of God doesn't work that way; it leads and guides us daily into all truth. The truth is what sets people free from decisions that they can't decide on at the time.

We need to make decisions that involve what's important to the path we take. When the right direction of that decision has been made, it will set you free. You won't feel like you made the wrong decision based on somebody else's reasoning where you may end up at your appointed time.

Change Your Appointment

Hebrew 9:27, "And as it is appointed unto men once to die, but after this judgement." One thing for certain and two things for sure, death and resurrection are sure to come and we will not miss that appointment because it has a destinated time set.

Have you ever experienced someone else making a decision for you and before you know it you question how did you get in that place?

Now you have to make the best of a situation you could have avoided by saying I'm not available, or I already have another appointment elsewhere. When you don't make your own decision or speak up for yourself, someone else will. Our choices are built on how much time we waste, and how much time we spend wisely on the choices we make as opposed to having someone else making a choice for us or not having our own agenda.

Would you rather spend your time on being the person you want to be or end up in the long run being disappointed that you didn't become the person you set out to be?

Do you want to end up being bitter in life because you haven't fulfilled anything you prayed for or long for? I don't say hope because hope deferred make the heart sick. Proverbs 13:12. When you read that scripture to the fullest, there is a desire and life that cometh.

In other words, something being delayed, hope for or the wrong desire in life can place you at a stand still position. Possibly bringing some of the things that you need fulfilled in your day to pass. When change takes place in some of our decisions, we have to adjust to the changes that need to be made and make the right choices that are beneficial.

At times, changing our direction can save our lives.

We receive God's desire for us to experience a fruitful life of love, joy, peace and righteousness in the Holy Ghost. By investing in our future, it can help lead us into making the right choices, or the wrong choices depending on who we're listening to.

Thank God we are not consumed by the cares of this world and others as we go on and live out our life based on His plans and purpose He has for our lives. "I know the thoughts I have towards you, thoughts of good and not evil that would bring to you an expected end". Jeremiah 29:11. A fulfillment, a completion. Do you hear that God has a perfect plan as He changes our direction?

Since we only have one life to live, choose wisely throughout the day, because within that very moment it can slip up on us before we know it. Anything can happen. It will show up when we least expect it, as once stated, "in a twinkling of an eye." We will stand face-to-face with God who will ask us to give an account for ourselves and explain what and how we have been living our life out here on earth.

This is not intended to frighten you, but to enlighten us to choose our time wisely because every one of us shall give an account of himself to God before the great white throne. It's doesn't matter if we are pleasing one another while here on earth trying to make sure were living a Holy life before one another; it's our relationship that we have in Christ and how we please him.

One thing about this relationship with God is that He's everywhere and ever present. He sits high and looks low. He knows every hair on our head. Every time we say, "I can do it later" or "I don't have time for that now" we put ourselves on God's time table and movement in our lives. How and where He plan for us to live out our life for eternity.

Is this about one another yes and no? No. This is strictly about living our lives pleasing before Him.

We all have an option to choose how we live and how we go before Him seeking His direction of our whereabouts. We don't want to live our lives in regret. It's never too late to make a change and stay on the path that has been designed and designated for your purpose.

Are we exempt from such distraction that might invade our path? No.

As we travel along life's way, they may come to deter us, to alter our steps in a place, a different direction that will keep us from accomplishing our goals. Yes, they are called distractions and little foxes that suddenly appear at different times an seasons in our life.

Hidden thoughts that eat after our hearts, wills and emotions stop us from fulfilling what we really set out to fulfill in different times in our lives. Since our heart is filled with the issues of life, based on our personal motives, purpose, and intention, God's will concerning our path, goals and purposes, will keep us out of areas that have no real meaning for the desires we set out to fulfill.

Every day of our lives, we wake up to another shifting in the atmosphere. We make up in our minds that what we planned to do in our day (by commanding our morning, changing our direction, creating new and witty ideas), is something from which we can benefit. We can be successful if we don't allow doubt to creep in and turn us into another direction.

Anytime we allow guilt, worry, fear, anxiety, jealousy, envy and greed to slip in, it complicates our thought patterns, which take prevalence over our day and time. Take charge over your thoughts that come to complicate your decisions you have authority over what come to set up space in your mind.. A lot of negative imagination along with those things mentioned above invites themselves in without an invitation, and we must keep our thoughts from being marred by the attack of the devil. I know you might say, "It's not always the devil."

The attack on any unwavering thought is of the devil and self-control is an imperative role that needs to awaken your spirit so you can make that change and seize your day and live out your day on purpose.

Planning out your day before your feet hit the floor is imperative. It's like having a lamentation moment, "God's mercy is new every morning." Lamentation 3:22-23. Take out some time and just lay prostrate in your bed meditating on your next move. After you get up, sit on the edge of the bed and start talking to your feet telling them, "You're going in the right direction today". Plan your day by going before God and asking Him for guidance. "Seeking first the kingdom of God" is a commandment. Listen to the guided directive it is giving out because you never know on any given day what you may experience.

The path you may take may be closed, or an accident may have occurred before you got there; don't be so quick to move your feet in a direction that you didn't take time out to seek God's will and purpose for in your day.

Our life choices on how we spend our time can become hectic making doctor appointments, hair appointments, nail appointments, planning our children's activities, etc. How much of that time do we end up having a feeling of regret because we didn't get a chance to fulfill all that we set out to do? When we change our direction and seek out God's direction, He gives us grace to live one day at a time. Apart from God, we can't do anything (John 15:5). The best choice you can make each day is to begin that day and time with God.

Here's another storyline about what I've been thinking lately. It was based on me making the right decision one day.

The Right Decision

This started within an experience I had with a friend of mine.

Her: How are you I'm having an event that is very important and I hope you can make.

Me: I'm not going to be able to make your special day, but I will get with you and bless you tremendously. You know I'm excited about this wonderful elevation that is taking place in your life, but I cannot be pulled into two directions." I'd already committed myself to this other engagement that had prevalence over this appointment.

Her: Well I pray you find time because, this is very special to me

Me: You know God spoke a word of truth through you when He allowed you to post on facebook, *"One direction."* on facebook on my wall. When I saw it, confirmation struck my thoughts and the first thing that came from it helped me to make the right decision (although my decision was not satisfactory to her).

Her: Just pray about it, talk to you soon…(with attitude.)

Me: I know you might not understand this, but I had to make the right decision for me. I must inform you that I am heading in the right direction and the right decision was made for me on that same day.

Even though our appointments were scheduled at the same time, I had to choose what was right for me and make the right decision within that day. Like Elijah when he was wavering between two opinions (1 King 18:21); he came and to all the people and asked, "How long will ye halt ye between two opinions. If the Lord be God follow him but if it be Baal, then follow him and they answered him not a word".

So that day, even though it may have cost me my relationship with my sister in Christ, the right decision had to be made; I chose what was beneficial to me. Of, course she was not happy about my decision and still unhappy about the decision I had to make until this day.

Unfortunately, there happened to be two events going on at the same date and time and I needed to make the right decision that day to fulfill the proper obligation concerning me within that day. I could not be halted between opinions. I made the right decision that was beneficial for me.

What I don't appreciate with people who have appointments or engagements (that want your attendance at their functions) is when they inform you of them at the last minute – as if you're not doing anything with your life. Just because, I may not inform you of my whereabouts of my affairs does not mean I'm not engaged with other activities.

Remember, the steps of a good man is always ordered by the Lord and He is delighted in this way. Psalms 37:23. God is pleased when we make the right decision regardless of how someone else may feel because you choose yourself over them. And He takes great pleasure in blessing us when we walk upright before Him. God makes no mistakes in your day because you sought Him out first to help you make the right decision.

When you seek ye first the kingdom of God and all His righteousness, all the right decisions are made; you'll walk in the right way and He will always direct your path.

The truth sets us free when the right decision is made.

When we seek God and choose the direction He chose for us, everything else will fall in place. My decision was made and I was headed in the right direction that God set out for me to make that day. Making the right decision helped to set me free for every other decision I need to make throughout my life. It helped me complete some goals I had been praying for and had been setting aside just to please others. By trying to please others, you neglect to complete your plans and purposes concerning your life.

At the end of that conversation, I stated, "I pray you enjoy your next movement in your life because apparently this was the right decision for the course of your next level in your life. Don't get left behind because somebody else is not there to support you." Those were my encouraging words to her to help move her towards her destiny.

CHAPTER SIX

Being Outside Of Your Comfort Zone

Wind chasing the deer as he panteth in search of the water brooks. This phrase gets me every time I hear it. It's called a "deer's suicide," A deer was born to run free. Deers are not aware of their surroundings or the dangers that are centered in their path which they run through. They mostly chase the wind and sound they hear as they pants after the water brooks.

As human beings, we must be aware of our surroundings and the tactics of the wicked ones. We fall right into certain obstacles that may endanger us on our paths by not listening to the voice of God.

As a deer pants towards the water brooks, they may exactly run outside their safety zone and get struck by a car or truck because they are not aware of the tactic they may encounter along the way.

So, I wouldn't look at it as a suicidal incident as opposed to them being outside of their safety zone.

Have you heard of this song or scripture? "As the (hart) deer panteth for the water so my soul (my heart), longeth after thee". Psalm 42:1.

Deer are prone to long for water after they are being chased by a predator. In which we will call the enemy (Satan). As our souls long after thee; there are preventive measures setup by God for us to miss, such as; an accident, or some type of occurrence that may attack us. Some of us are not going to opt out by committing suicide as some that have gone on before us.

Unfortunately, when the deer is running free, he runs into an obstacle that endangers his surroundings and gets caught up in a snare – a trap that has been designed and set up by man (such as a highway or road). The deer gets caught up in the middle of the road that he must try to pass through to get to the other side. Now they're labeled as suicidal deer as if the deer intentionally tried to take their own lives. It's a setup, because the deer could not escape the trap that was set before them because they were created to run free.

This can also be considered a roadblock, something set up to keep us from moving ahead into our next destiny. Deers were created to be free…not to be trapped into man's snares.So are we. We were created to be free as it is stated, "Whom the son set free is free indeed".

We're not to be stopped or trapped into what man has created or fall into the snares of the enemy. You must declare, "I am no longer bound by the snares and traps by man. I am free indeed. It's turning around for my good".

It's Turning Around for My Good

It's turning around to them who searched out the richness of God's expectation in the kingdom of God. In the kingdom of God, billionaires are being raised up, for such a time as this. There's a supernatural shifting and God is speaking it with a still small voice.

It's going to spring forth in the right season.

Spiritual Nuggets: Right here is a very important prophetic revelation; there is an appointment for execution that is about to take place in the congregation of the people of God. A divine fulfillment of God's promises is getting ready to set the captives free.

In Due Season: If you faint not, you should reap that in which you have sowed. This year of 2019, this year and in this very hour, in this year, in this moment and in this day the promises and blessings of God is springing forth. Not last year 2018 blessings; but, 2018 blessings have rolled over into 2019. This year 2019, blessings are already in preparation for the next year 2020. The breakthroughs and blessings we are about to receive within the next (6) months. God has shifted us into the New Year already. We are now living in an open heaven and an open door that no man can close. God is getting ready to pour out blessings that you won't have room to receive.

This is not the time to be weary in your well doings. When you are doing well and being lined up with the instructions that are being given to you by God, and the man or woman of God that speaks a prophetic promise of prosperity over your life, hearken unto their voice. They are going to activate the manifestation of the supernatural breakthroughs that God has promised you through their prophetic authority given to them by God,

Even, in the church you may be now attending right now, you should reap a harvest if you faint not. You are now about to reap the benefits from what you have sown in the past and most recently. You have seed in the ground, now it's time to speak to your seed and say, "Return to me and that right soon according to the will and purposes of God's plans concerning my seed in the ground. I speak to my seed and therefore, tell my seed to go and grow, increase and return to me again that right soon". It will be given back to you according unto the faith you have been sowing into. Also, according to the measure of your day in which you search out the things of God by putting him first in everything you do from this day forward. As you are reading this material, I don't care what time of day or night you pick it up, what year or month that you pick it up.

Know that God is speaking to you concerning your seed. Know that God is speaking to you concerning prosperity. Know that God is speaking to you concerning your provision. Know that God is speaking prophetic prophecy over your life concerning your seed sown. Amen!

God has Set up a Remnant of People

God moves in agreement with us when we stay lined up with being in His presence with spiritual tools He provide; such as restoration, knowledge and truth. I am rich; my life shall now be exposed. My life is on the mantle that others have not seen a glimpse of His glory, purposes and plans He has prepare for me. In this season of my life. I walked therein, you need to reassure, yourself I will rise up, but not in distress. I will walk up victoriously while God uphold me into my destiny.

However, it may appear.

God feels your heart, pray for yourself and shut the lion's mouth. You are not forsaken, nor in despair. Speak a word over your life, "I am healed. I am delivered. I am set free. I am whole. God is working it out for my good." God is your deliverer. He has brought you out, so walk in your victory. "I'm clearing up your pathway. You're no longer like a deer panting after the water; you are a deer that is running free. I'm giving you a way of escape." said the Lord.

God has a remnant of people that he has lined up for such a time as this. He is calling them out by their name, as He did it in the garden when He called out Adam. He is turning things around for your good. This year of blessing is just the beginning of what's about to take place. Get ready for the roll-call. Keep your ear gate open. Don't get distracted by what you hear or see. Don't get distracted by what's going on, on your job, in your family, with this world system or social media. Get in place and position yourself to hear the voice of God.

A call of salvation is issued unto those that God has set apart; the saved one's that are called by His name will be saved. Those that confess with their mouth that Jesus is LORD, and that He is the King of Kings.

There is a remnant of people that will hear His voice and humble themselves under the mighty hand of God to live separated from this world. Just because we're in this world, does not mean we are of this world. "Be not conformed to this world but be ye transformed by the renewing your mind." Those people that are called by His name, He will rise them up in their rightful places. God is extending an invitation. Will you come to receive the word of God?

Receive and Believe it and get in a place to have a pen as a ready writer, to hear and write down everything that God is speaking to you in this season about. What is on your mind? What is in your hand? What have you been thinking lately? Set yourself apart by getting in place to receive what God is saying to you.

Although it's been delayed, it will not be denied. You may not have it at this moment, but this year is not over yet and He's turning it around for your good.

Now go, and collect your goods.

CHAPTER SEVEN

Go And Collect Your Goods

In 2 Chronicles 20, when Jehoshaphat and his people came to take their spoils, they found much among them including goods, garments and valuable things, which they took for themselves more than they could carry and they were three days taking the spoiled because there was so much.

Say this with me, "God is more than enough". Go and collect all your (spoils) pieces, pursue and take it all; for you should surely overtake and surely rescue. And, the Lord has given his people favor in the sight of the Egyptians so that they could have their request; Exodus 12:36

"Make your requests known unto to me", God said, "I will fulfill it". All the things you've been praying for, God has heard your request. Your prayers are not returning to God void. The last two times the Lord's words were spoken, He told you, "Though you be tried in the fire and your trials came to overtake you, embrace your challenges you shall overcome them. I am preparing a way of an escape for you. Therefore, know that no temptation, problem, situation, circumstance, nothing on your job, nothing concerning your family, nothing concerning sicknesses, none of these things will harm you. All of this has been placed in the palm of my hands. No man can pluck you out of my hand. Any circumstances that will rise up and try to override you. You will override and overtake them resist the devil and he shall flee."

Sometimes life challenges come to redirect our paths and it helps us to continue to pursue after the things we desire the most. Such as our goals, purposes and destiny. It helps us to seek and pursue God the more when we find ourselves in situation that is beyond our control. It places us before God kneeling before Him, asking Him for His help to redirect our steps. How many of you heard, "Trouble don't last always because God is always present in the times of our trouble"? Right in the challenges we face on a day-to-day basis. He's ever present and He hears and comforts us in our time of need.

"I have heard your prayers that you have petitioned and written down before me. Now, it's time to reap what you have sown your harvest is now I have seen the seeds that you have laid and planted before me and just like Jehoshaphat and his army arrived to collect their goods, within three days you are going to collect all that you have sown and more." said the Lord.

The word of God that has been spoken over your life prophetically over the last three years or more stating more than enough is getting ready to drop with fatness. I want you to pray on the behalf of all the churches where people are attending throughout this nation and I declare your prophetic breakthrough of more than enough is showing up today.

When David inquired of the Lord saying what shall I pursue after this troop? Shall I overtake them? And he answered David, "Pursue; for thou shalt surely overtake them and without fail recover all". I Samuel 30:8

This particular message came through to me while watching the transformers and once they thought that they destroyed one of the transformers he continued to fight and move about his enemies to collect his pieces his (goods). He began to reform back into the image and likeness of what he was created to be and he was able to stand in the midst of them until his help came forth (through) to help him defeat his enemies. We got some enemies that we need some help to fight off, we're calling forth some prayer warriors to help us to defeat some trails and tribulations we find ourselves in. One will chase ten thousand and two will send ten thousand or more to flight encouraging you that you are not alone. As it is stated in Deuteronomy 30:32.

That's when it leaped in my spirit to get up and get my ready pen and start writing down what the spirit of God was saying. Though your enemy came in like a flood, I'm going to build a standard against them and give you the power to overtake them.

You often time here you need not to fight in this battle, that this battle is not yours to fight. Stand still and see the salvation of the LORD move on your behalf. I will fight this battle for you vengeance is mine said the LORD. Some battles require your attention and you must fight the good fight of faith, and show forth your authority and take it by force in the kingdom of God. But the majority of times you must stand still and be quite. That's when you can see the salvation of God moving on your behalf knowing that all things are working together for your good. Every argument is not your fight, every circumstance that comes to try to hinder you from exiting through your next entrance into your future, continue to move forward, pursue it and conquer it all.

Therefore, know that there's a war going on and you must fight to gain the victory over your situation, over your circumstance, over your husband and what he's battling with every demonic spirit that is overriding his mind to make him think that he has to continue in pornography, sexual promiscuous spirits that attack him in his night season.

You must fight that battle that is wrestling with your wife that continues to come to make her think that you are having an affair outside of your home with some other woman functioning out of a spirit of infidelity. You must fight to believe that your children are going to be delivered from drugs and alcohol and from this new marijuana that is running rapid and out of control, In the name of

Jesus. You must fight for your job when they are coming up against you, when a group of people have come up against you and lied on you, you must fight to believe that your children and your children's children are going to become entrepreneurs and have business plans, you must fight for these things in the name of Jesus.

When you hear a time to sow a gift sow your best seed because it's time to reap your harvest in this season you are going to collect your seed you have sown.

Whatever, year you find yourself in, that's the year you will reap if you faint not. It appears that you have been giving more than you've been receiving, rest assure everything that has been stolen, lost or taken from you. God is getting ready to release your harvest that you've sown your prayers are getting ready to be answered, your children, children's children will be delivered from gun violence; things will begin to turn around for your good today and before this year out go and collect your goods.

There was so much that it took three days just to collect it all.

Jehoshaphat and his army arrived to collect the spoils from the war they discovered there it were far more good, garments and more, don't look no longer at the spoils as if something has been spoiled or gone bad but, look in the eyes of God that provides nothing but the best. The Lord our God is preparing a good ground for your harvest.

Reap What You Have Sown

While journaling through the greatest novel ever written the Bible in the Book of Psalms in chapter 126. I stumbled upon these two verses my soul started rejoicing and God's word started speaking to my spirit (my inward man) and at that very moment'; I started thanking God for his confirmation though this scripture. They that sown in tears shall reap in Joy, he that goeth forth and wept bearing precious seed, shall doubtless come again with rejoicing, bringing his sheaves with him.

Have you ever heard this song "bringing in the wheat, bringing in the wheat early in the morning? Bringing in the wheat? But, have you ever really looked over the words and knew actually what they were singing, some of us probably thought that it was some old country tell song? That didn't have much intentions half of us thought they were saying "bring in the sheep". But, God that brings forth much revelation about sowing and reaping a harvest, also gives you understanding

Just look over these words in this song:

Sowing in the morning, sowing seeds of kindness, sowing in the noontide and the dewy eve; waiting for the harvests, and the time of reaping. We shall come rejoicing, bringing in the sheaves.

Bringing in the sheaves, bringing in the sheaves. We shall come rejoicing bringing in the sheaves. Bringing in the sheaves, bringing in the sheaves, we shall come rejoicing, bringing in the sheaves. Sowing in the sunshine, sowing in the shadows, fearing neither clouds nor winter's chilling breeze; by and by the harvest and the labor ended, we shall come rejoicing, bringing in the sheaves (wheat).

Overflow

Then I heard overflow I got too shouting, singing and I said well, well, well; let's see what the word of the Lord is saying through this scripture for it is written; search the scriptures daily for in them you find life; but, it doesn't say that he said you 'think' you find life. So, in this very hour the word of the Lord was saying be 'steadfast unmovable always abounding in the work of the Lord and you should weep if you faint not," meaning that He is true to his word and He said it, if I promise it, I'm going to also establish it and it shall come to pass. Wait on it don't be alarmed don't be shaken. You shall reap a harvest from the seeds you have sown, thou they are delayed they shall show up in due season.

Spiritual nugget: for surely life bringeth forth light that shineth through God's people even in the darkness.

Spoken March 13, 2017; the LORD will perfect that which concerned me.

LORD, give your people a heart of worship that they may be saved.

A liar lies, a cheater cheats a thief steals.

Spoken March 11, 2017; living a life of freedom and not knowing or recognizing that your freedom requires some time out.

Always abounding in the things of the Lord, be ye ever ready to give an account for your actions speak louder than your words, for faith without works is dead.

The well is running dry the people are thirsty go and refill the water pots, let them overflow. The church is out of touch, the people are searching and looking for another movement from the inside out. They are showing up on Sundays in their church home where they attend and leaving out running into another church looking to hear a word or looking for another outpouring to satisfy their longings, instead of seeking the kingdom of God in the place where he has assigned them to. So, that all these things can be added unto them that they are seeking elsewhere. If they would just be still at their home inside their own church for a little while longer. They would hear what the spirit has to say to the church which is living within their spirit man and n their inward parts.

Read and search the scriptures daily "for in them you think you find life." Here are a couple of scriptures to read at your leisure

1st Corinthians 15:58: be ye steadfast

Matthew 24:44: be ever ready always abounding

Matthew 12:36: everyone will have to give an account for their actions

James 2:26: faith without works is dead

Where Art Thou?

God has been calling you by your name. God is saying; where are you in this hour and in this time of season of your life. The kingdom of God is at hand and the time has come for you to shake off every wind and doctrine of your past encounters and start living in the Kingdom of God. Mark 1:15

A time of refreshing has come for you to receive your compensation, your rewards from your sowing and weeping. You must clear up every debt you owe and repent of any and all unknown or known unclean thoughts that you have towards one another to regain your profit from your labor. In Proverbs 14:24: there is a profit for the people of God, but you must be found in your rightful place, position yourself. Every year we enter into another level being in another place of worship going from glory to glory, to another level of praise.

Even the church at larges is now evolving into a different level of principles, directives and instructions coming from the knowledge of the kingdom of God at hand. This is the outpouring of the

Kingdom of Heaven it is so powerful during this season of our life some of us will miss it if we're not in our rightful place here on earth.

God is looking for his people that is showing up in the kingdom of God so that he can compensate them, bless them in this season of atonement, repentance and fulfillment you will be rewarded for this in your due season don't get weary in well-doing. You should reap if you faint not Galatians 6:9, there should be a performance Luke 1:45; we are going to reap our benefits or rewards based on how we serve God here on earth.

Where are you? Don't get caught up with the cares of this world, cast all your cares on me said the Lord Psalms 55:23, God is searching out the earth for his righteous people that will not stagger at his promises.

Abraham, believed in the Lord and he counted it to him for righteousness, Genesis 15:6; he was found giving glory to God and being fully persuaded. He was able to perform the righteousness of God.

Throughout your daily meditation attached these scriptures to the following storylines that you have going through your mind and what you have been thinking lately, such as: Psalm 55:23; Cast thou burdens upon the Lord and he shall sustain thee, and he shall never suffer the righteous to be moved.

Now let's look at the word "sustain," he will support you. He will supply your every need with substance. Every seed you have sown you shall receive a profit for God is not slack in his promise. Psalm 68:19; blessed be the Lord who daily loaded us with benefits.

Let's look at the word "loaded," noted as an example of searching out the entire scripture what it means to hear the word loaded us; one will think of providing all of our finances, food on the table, clothes and shoes to wear. But it actually means to bear our burdens, casting all our cares upon him, because he will supply all of our needs as we seek ye first the kingdom of God. That whatsoever, we bear or loadeth down with all these things will be added unto us.

At times, being in the need of those things can become a heavy burden when you don't have it, God daily loads us with benefits.

And, if he promises it, we will receive a profit.

Looking at the word "benefits:" meaning a payment or gift, as one made to help someone or something given by an employer.

Amen, to God be the Glory.

CHAPTER EIGHT

Release God's Glory

The levels of God's glory over your life and his purpose of his glory is being revealed and will forever be distinguished by your faith.

Your entry into your next level depends on where you see yourself from this year out. Your entrance into your New Year is preparing you because your time is now and it has finally come to test your faith level in God.

You must walk by faith and not by sight it's nothing wrong with your vision you just need a clearer vision from what you've been seeing. Remain focused on the things of God, channel into his 20/20 vision. Pray for the seven eyes of God. Revelation 5:6 and I behold and lo, in the midst of the throne and to the four beasts and in the midst of the elders stood a lamb as it has been slain having seven horns and seven eyes which are the seven spirits of God sent forth into all the earth.

Zechariah 3:9; upon one stone shall be seven eyes. Zechariah 4:1; they are the eyes of the Lord, which run to and forth throughout the whole earth.

They are eyes that have not seen nor, ears heard all of the glorious things God is getting ready to unfold. God is speaking His words they are now coming alive in you on the things you have studied to show yourself approved. Every word that you have applied to your life from hearing the word of God from Sunday to Sunday and weekdays to weekdays every prayer night you attended and that you have failed to show up for.

Let's not forget Bible study.

God wants his glory to shine forth in you like never before. God's glory is an illumination of his wonderous power being revealed and manifested in your life through his miracles, signs and wonders shining forth through you. We are not ashamed of the Gospel of Jesus Christ for it is the power of salvation. Romans 1:16

Let the glory of God shine forth in you now so you can enter into the New Year covered under the glory cloud. The glory cloud can become so thick it becomes like a mist or fog that will fill the temple with praise. The presence of God will come in and take over the entire room it will captivate the people's heart. There is a glory train like the tail of a bride's gown walking down the aisle of the sanctuary.

You've heard of this statement, let the glory train fill this temple.

One of the glory trains could be considered as "the Lord is my banner" known as Jehovah Nissi. He will cover us from generation to generation to come. Exodus 17:15-16; the Lord high and lifted up and his train filled the temple, Isaiah 6:1 or Ezekiel 10:4; for the glory of the Lord rose from the cloud and filled the temple; 2nd Chronicles 5:14 put it this way the glory of the Lord filled the temple that the people went up with praise. Amen!

Spiritual nuggets: Angels unaware you provide angels unaware to shield and protect us from all harm and danger. You oh God is adored forever above the universe; you give us everlasting joy full of hope and glory. Oh God, for that I should thank you Lord for everything.

Spoken October 20, 2015; I decree and declare this, I break the backbone of every demonic force of the wicked hearsays and naysayers. In Jesus name! every tongue that rise up against me in judgement God said he will condemn it; you will condemn it.

No weapon formed against me shall prosper

And I quote, "You will get this after a while," Apostle Marshall Davis.

Release God's Glory

The effectual fervent prayers of the righteous man availeth much. Behold, I received a commandment to bless: and he hath blessed;

and I cannot reverse it Numbers 23:20. The blessing of God is overtaking you at this very hour the blessing of God that make you rich and add no sorrow. Proverbs 10:22

The word blessings have been flowing out of your mouth for the last two months. This word is a confirmed word and it has been established keep activating it with your voice; blessings, blessings and blessings over your finances, over your health, in your home and on your job. This confirmed word will be established and it will not return unto me void said the Lord, I don't care what it looks like at this very moment in your life it cannot be reversed it shall come to pass. Stand firm on the promises of God's blessings and more blessings will be coming your way and that right soon.

You have been faithful over a few things and because of your faithfulness and your obedience unto me says the Lord, I am carrying out a good work in you and you shall receive your breakthrough before this year end. I'm talking about the year you're in now a right now supernatural breakthrough is breaking forth in this season of your life.

I heard your cry said the Lord, I heard your voice, I heard your shout of blessings, blessings, blessings and more blessings send forth your blessings now God. We are in need of a breakthrough now. God, we need a manifestation of your miracle, signs and wonders now. Send forth your healing power now God, have your way now God, in our church, in our home, in our community, with our city, birthing of new businesses, send your blessings on our jobs now Lord and bless our children now. Oh God, we need you to show forth thy manifestation of thy breakthroughs now, your supernatural healing now.

We're calling those things forth as though they were now. Thank you in advance God for the manifestation of your confirmed word through your inspired men and women you have placed before us even in this hour in our life and for such a time as this. God thank you for bringing it to pass and for not letting your words return unto you void. If you said that you will perform it then there should be a performance of those things that God has spoken unto his people.

We should reap what we have sown over our seeds that have already been planted in the ground. It will grow up as a supernatural abundance seed planted in the ground to spring forth in its due season. That is going to show forth as a supernatural abundance breakthroughs throughout this nation, throughout this world and throughout all churches at large. Throughout this universe your people will be sharing your blessings with one another thanking you in advance for enlarging our territory.

The power of the prayers of Jabez will come alive once again in the people of God's heart as they decree and declare; oh, that you may enlarge my territory once again and send forth your increase where no evil can not harm me.

God, we thank you for blessing seen and unseen blessings. We sit down and ponder over our thoughts on a day-to-day basis over things that are good and those things that are bad, and we have develop a pattern of saying hate those things that are evil and love those things that is good; that end up developing negative thoughts to arise until we don't know which way to turn. Then go into the word and recite, "if I be not angry and sin not and don't let the sun go down on my head, then there will be no wrath upon my head." God will redeem me. But, So, a person can be mad, upset and angry all day until midnight repent wake up with that same attitude or behavior? Not so.

Forgive us when we take your word out of content and use it against one another in a selfish way. Forgive us when we don't trust you enough when we think on those things that are negative towards one another that be going on in our head. When we should be thinking on those things which are lovely, just and pure, honest and if there be any virtue to think on those things. When we don't take the time out to meditate as often as we should.

When we should be taking out some real time out to write those thoughts down. Going forward " indicting our tongue as having a pen as ready writer," that will help our enlarge our way of thinking to help those who are willing and obedient to their cause to write out the storyline that theyve been wanting to share with others. What is on there heart to write about. There's a book within you write the vision make it plain for those that read it those that run with it will be held responsible of their own actions.

Continue to trust in the Lord with all thy heart and lean not unto thy own understanding for, the Lord said he takes great pleasure in blessing his people. God said I will bless you going in and going out God hears our prayers, God hears our thoughts, God see us writing down what's on our mind, what we've been thinking lately. Who we have been thinking about, if God has been putting people in front of you and you see the faces of people then all of a sudden you should just start praying for that person and when they see your face they should be praying for you as well?

God have commanded us to pray for one another and to encourage one another, build one another up just be in the presence of God and know that God is listening to you when you speak out loud as I said earlier in the book. God is waiting for your voice activation he wants to hear from you he said my sheep hear my voice and no other they will follow.

God, wants to hear from you God don't want you to do all the talking he wants to have a conversation with you. He wants you to get in a place where you can be positioned enough to have a time of meditation, a time of consecration, a time to lay before him when you're sitting in the house, its not always in front of the television, its not always listening to music, its not always about having company all the time and being on the telephone we say guard our ear gate, their so many voices out there but, we continue to let them speak in our earor listen to the many voices that may deter us from our purpose.

Sometimes our company is a big distraction to what it is that we should be doing in our house especially when our house is not clean.

The very people you chose to let sit around in your house are the very ones that is going outside your house saying child I was over what's her name house and she didn't get up and clean up at all. What's her name was too busy trying to entertain you. How did you leave your house, your house probably wasn't clean when you left?

You probably need to go back and clean up your own house.

You heard the saying; sweep around your own front door before you sweep around mine.

Then stop being so easily distracted by entertaining others and be obedient unto the voice of God. In your faithfulness I will bless you I will give you a continual overflow, I will increase you and enlarge your territory. This is just the beginning of your time invested in me through your prayers interceding on the behalf of others. I will call on the intercessors all over the world from the east, north, south and west to call out your name for your blessings to come and knock on the door of your soul, your soul belongs to me therefore I will bless you from this day forever more.

Stand still and see the salvation of God move on your behalf today though the effectual fervent prayers of the righteous man that availeth much.

Pray without Ceasing II

Praise God lets get right into prayer. How many know that faith is the key in prayer unlocks the door? How many of you heard that phrase to find out if it was true or not?

Everything you hear most of the time is being paraphrased and you must study to show yourself approved did you \ know that faith is the key that unlocks the doors and prayer is the functionality of what we should be doing to activate or bring it into fruition. It's the same thing with this particular passage "if my people, which are called by my name shall humble themselves and pray and seek my face and turn from their wicked ways then will I hear from heaven and I will forgive their sin and will heal their land." 2nd Chronicles 7:14

The key note here is "if my people" God is stating something there, he's speaking to a "remnant of people" that is called by his name. Therefore, means some people are not called by His name. Another, point He's making in this passage is "and turn from their evil ways: meaning that there are some evil people that are still functioning out of evil. So, therefore, we must search every word spoken and study it for ourself to see how and what is relating to concerning God's will for our life. As if, we have become scientist to dissect the true meaning of what the word is saying concerning us. Not just show up for church on Sunday looking for a prophetic word spoken over your life from someone else. The key passage here is "study to show yourself approve." We'll dissect that another time.

Everything you pray for in this season during seed, sowing and harvest time God is going to reveal his plan concerning you. He's going to release abundance of favor over your life. Through faith being the substance of things hoped for and the evidence of all that you have set your heart out to pray for shall come to pass.

Faith is the Key

Let's look at the phrase prayer being the key and faith unlocking the doors. Now ask yourself, why wouldn't prayer be the key as opposed to faith being the key?

Prayer is defined as speaking or communicating with God. For a person to pray there must be one on one an acknowledgement of God's existence. The key will not exist without God being God who is the creator of all things. He made the key so that our prayers through faith will unlock the doors. You can have a key to a house or to a car but if they are not the right set of keys you cannot enter that car or the house.

Faith is belief, confidence, trust and reliance. Faith is the key that unlocks many doors that are connected to Heaven through your prayers and the Lord God himself is the key that is needed to see the things behind the closed doors, that we cannot see without this key you cannot open these doors. Faith without works is dead so if, you don't have the proper key you don't have no works.

Another way to study a word that is being recited in a message, is to line it up with the scripture. Every passage of phrase and all phrases that is spoken over your life should normally be backed up with scripture. Or do you just believe what everyone else is saying instead of searching out the meaning of the scripture for yourself

I hear some of you out there right now saying what is she talking about. I hear this a lot, my general response would be, the reason you can't comprehend what it is I'm saying is because if you don't read and you don't study the scripture for yourself to know where its coming from, how could you know what I'm talking about.

For it is written; with all thy getting get an understanding. We often times hear prayer is the key that unlocks the doors and think that what it says, until I look it up myself, I thought so too. But, its actually "faith is the key that unlocks the door."

Most of the time when you read something for yourself when He said write the vision and make it plain so that those that read it can receive it and comprehend it with and understanding can also gain from it.

Here's another statement I hear all the time. Well are you going to talk about prayer and teach at the same time, 'my respons.' I'm going to do them both? What's on your mind about this?

Before you can get into prayer you should pick out a scripture for each thing you plan to pray about and use it as an entrance to your prayer as the key. When we pray, we pray for certain things and we should be praying Gods words and not just using phrases or quotes from what we've heard from other people and what they are saying.

If you study to show yourselves approved then we can equip ourselves to be ready to say what "thus says the Lord' at all times to speak the word of God and not always say what you heard.

The main thing is to say what the word says. If, you're not reading his word for yourself or studying to show yourself approved a workman that need not be ashamed but rightly dividing in the word of truth; then you're listening to someone else again.

A lot of us don't pray according to the word of God because we are not studying or setting ourselves aside to read God's word or scripture for ourselves so that we can form them in our prayer life, such as; this particular scripture. With Gods stripes I am healed with Gods stripes you are healed. With his stripes God said you were healed. Immediately when he went to the cross, he bored all our sicknesses on the cross. Do you believe what I'm saying or do you believe what you're saying through your confession and voice activation?

It behooves me, when I hear people say they don't know how to pray. What on earth got you this far in life, its truly not based off someone else's prayer. Although, you often hear this phrase "somebody prayed for me they had me on their mind they took the time to pray for me. I'm so glad they prayed, I'm so glad they prayed for me.

We are intercessor praying all over the world that we are being summoned for, from the east, north, south and west to pray on the behalf of other's needs. Our prayers are going forth because everybody needs prayer to set themselves apart and cry out to God and say 'it's me oh Lord standing in the need of prayer' not my mother, not my father nor my sister nor my brother. It's not my children, not my job, but its me oh Lord seeking your face concerning my issues that is going on in my life. Be open and be honest before the LORD and tell him you need help and you are in need of a breakthrough.

I'm in need of a favor, I need some doors opening for me. I need a supernatural abundance of prosperity breakthrough overflowing in my life. I need to know that you hear my voice when I come before you day and night seeking your face crying out before you.

This is the kind of conversation that you want to be having when you go before God. These are the kind of thoughts that should be running through your mind. You can't allow the devil to come and make you afraid to open up your mouth because of your past failures or doubts.

Activate your voice so God can hear you stop looking for somebody else to pray for you.

Yes, it's written, if there's any amongst you that are sick let them call on the elders of the church, yes, it's written; healing is the children's bread. But when are you going to use that word for yourself? How much are you talking that thing out for yourself with God day and night? How much are you laying hands upon your body, upon your knees, upon your back, upon your head for yourself? How much of your deliverance do you see working and moving on your behalf when your car needs to be fixed, when your mortgage needs to be paid, when your car note need to be paid, when your insurance need to paid.

Who have you been talking to concerning fulfilling those things that is needed in your life?

As we continue to go on and a we continue to go forth and further on into prayers that you have been praying. Start speaking scriptures over them which is the word of God and don't listen to the voices that say anybody can quote a scripture over and over again. That's good, scriptures are the word of God written for that situation that is going on in your life. Don't let anyone discourage you about reciting them over and over again.

When you speak the word of God know that you are rebuking every foul spirit that come against you by speaking the word of God over it. Cast down that spirit and command that spirit to dry up and die through the word of God. Amen!

Prayer is and will always open the door to the heart God to attend His helping hand.

Faith will always remain the key that activate the prayers and His blessing to overflow and overtake you. 'Because he loves me says the Lord, I will rescue him; I will protect him; I will be with him in the time of trouble, I will deliver him and honor him. With long life will I satisfy him and show him my salvation. Psalms 91:14-16.

Lets pray today for the peace of God on our lives and throughout this world for this hour till we meet again Number 6:24. "the Lord bless you and keep you may the Lord make his face to shine upon you and be gracious to you and may he turn his face towards you and give you peace.

Spiritual Nuggets:

Please note one thing you don't always have to quote the exact address but you always must be ready to give an account to where it is located.

Walk in the light the beautiful light somewhere the dew drops of mercy shine bright, shine all around us both day and night Jesus the light of the world. Author Unknown

1 John 1:7: but if we walk in the light as he is in the light, we have fellowship one with another and the blood of Jesus Christ his son cleanses us from all sin.

Continuing with effectual prayers of a righteous man that availeth much:

Thank you God for supernatural breakthrough concerning salvation and deliverance. We trust you Lord as always and forever as you work things together for our good, we take nothing for granted we trust you as the head of everything and for every soul that belongs to you. Everything concerning our lives our thoughts and our decision making. We believe in supernatural things that passed all our understanding. Thank you for:

- Supernatural abundance
- Supernatural breakthroughs
- Supernatural miracles

Supernatural Healing:

Over our finances we pray for restoration over our family, friends and loved ones we see marriages being restored we pray for spiritual awakening among our children's, children's children's. Give us the power to decrease the onslaught of the enemy over the gun violence in this world we come against every attack that comes to destroy our economic stability over our nation and cities.

Supernatural riches are flowing from the heavenlies you said, let the poor say I am rich. We thank you for more God, we thank you for good and plenty. You supply all of our needs for the Lord is our shepherd and we should not want for anything; you open up doors that no man can close and you close doors that no man can open. We're living out of the supernatural abundance that you supply on a daily basis that confound the wise to say that God did it. It was God. We walk by faith and not by sight. We are walking in our supernatural breakthroughs today in the suddenly. You're providing a sudden breakthrough for jobs and better job funding for education.

We're connecting with intercessors to intercede all over this nation by the grace of God and we are calling those things forth as though they were, we coming against social media, over the airways for supernatural healing for our church, in our home on our jobs, in our marriage and over our relationships for one another. God, we're believing you for a supernatural revival to restore our finances for your people. In Jesus name and it is so.

Amen! After praying these prayers, you should have a testimony.

CHAPTER NINE

My Testimony

This is my testimony of where God has brought me from and I'm showing forth his promises unto me that I should weep a harvest if I faint not. Or, I should bring forth a harvest if I sow seed.

Just by taking God at his word and taking time out to study his word, I trust him in His word for his promises that has not always been a comfortable place for me. But, when I let go and let God, he always came forth to show himself approved and strong on my behalf.

He said they should weep as they go to plant their seed. They will sing as they returned with the harvest, he who has gone out weeping and bearing the seed of sewing should come home with shouts of joy caring sheaves with them.

Lets search out the meaning of sheaves again and its weeping what you have sown. That you've been interceding on the behalf of others, being kind and considerate having compassion for one another. God promise in his word you will and you shall see a performance of what you have sown.

Just recently I have been enlightened about sowing, its not about sowing into a person that is requesting a seed nor the amount being ask to sow rather its $100 seed or $100,000 dollar seed. It's about sowing into your future to reap what you have sown by sowing into into someone else's life or the kingdom of God in order to receive your harvest remember planting a small seed can give you a greater reward.

So don't let nobody discourage you about the seed that your sowing by faith. Trust God for the increase of that seed that you sowing within three days says the Lord you should reap what you have sown.

Remember the days of small beginnings always stands with a small gift usually all small seeds become the greatest gift. A seed of a mustard seed fate will grow richly in the ground.

God, I thank you in advance for giving me a clear understanding of your word to your scripture concerning small beginnings and reaping the harvest of what I have sown already. The song writer puts it this way "to reap what I 'have' sown" the key word here is 'have,' what you have already sown and you shall sow even a greater seed.

Days of Small Beginnings

The day of small beginnings which is considered small things is usually God's way to begin his great works in us with something if its just starting up a small businesses, getting a small house, buying a small cars. They will always increase into bigger and better cars a larger and better house or you becoming a CEO for a large business.

We often time hesitate to support one another in the fear of what others may say or think. The only things we should be concern about when it becomes about what other people think. We should be thinking on these things; whatsoever is lovely, whatsoever is pure, just, honest and if there be any virtue; think only that is good.

By sowing your seed this could be your breakthrough for when you need support in your business and by you helping someone else's dreams or ideas you can get the same support.

The days of small beginnings always starts with a small gift and usually our smallest gift become our greatest gift. I know that sounds like its repetitive but, listen to it starting with a small gift usually becomes our greatest gifts.

Confession

Confess your faults to the Lord dear Lord, I acknowledge all your blessings big and small but I just need a supernatural financial breakthrough to get through this financial setback that I'm in at this moment. I have made some mistakes and you were there before, everyday Lord you made a way out of no way.

That right there is considered a supernatural breakthrough.

As I continue to confess my need before God. I prayed; I need your help even now Lord more today than yesterday help me to see through this situation. Each difficult test and time in my life you've been there for me. God, I trust you Lord and I know it your will, that I may prosper before you. You will see me through this once again thank you Lord in the name of Jesus Christ, the son of the living God. Amen!

God you said you take great pleasure in blessing me.

Listen to what God said, that he takes great pleasure in blessing you but the only way that your going to receive that blessing is that you remind him of his words, you said that your word will not return back onto you void. God and you said that you take great pleasure and blessing me and I need you right now God to bless me with the things that I need to be taken care of in my life, even on this day.

Concerning my children, concerning my house, concerning my job, concerning the churches at large, concerning this world, concerning this nation. Lord God concerning the President, concerning the government.

God, I confess with my mouth that Jesus Christ is Lord that he died on the cross for my sins and he rose again on the third day and you said that you were going to open up doors that no man can open, God you said that you will help me. I believe that you are going to help me right now even as I say this prayer God. I extend a special prayer even for those that are getting ready to read this book oh God I thank you Lord Father God for giving them the strength and the courage to support me and be a blessing to me in the name of Jesus. I asked you to bless every hand that touch this book. Father God multiply the multiplication of their blessings Lord that they read it and go forth weeping and rejoicing bountifully from sowing their seed.

God begin a new life with those that have a new book in their heart, that they desire to get published or be a ready writer help them to set a new time of consecration before you in the name of Jesus to accomplishe it. Thank you for it right now.

Spiritual Nugget: Esteem One Another

Let us exalt one another daily and let nothing be done through strife or vain glory but in lowliness of mind let each of us esteem one another better than ourselves.

You should be conscious of your actions daily esteeming one another daily living in the now.

Testimony of Gratitude

Waking up with the testimony of God's wonderful breakthroughs on a daily basis helps to empower your mind to become free and bring you into repentance. A lot of times we don't give thanks as much as we ought too or testify how the Lord has set us free.

We shy away from testifying if we haven't been blessed with a new car, new house, new job or financial breakthroughs. So, we don't often stand up and tell of the goodness of Jesus and all that he has done for us on a regular basis

But how many can truly say that God blesses them daily to stand and say that God let me live to see another day, I'm grateful. That even though it's been delayed it will not be denied, I'm grateful just knowing that God is working those things together for my good. God kept me and he didn't let me fall, he kept me out of the hand of the wicked one.

God has opened many doors no man can close and many doors that no man can open; Revelation 3:8

I will testify every time I get a chance.

This is what we say not as often as we do from this day forth and forevermore. Every time I enter into his gate I will enter with a testimony of gratitude, with praise no matter how I'm looked upon because God has set me free from the bondage of death.

I'm kept in my right mind he didn't let sickness overtake me. He put food on my table today, He put clothes on my back today, I have legs to walk, shoes on my feet. Today he healed me from poverty, He's helping me to walk in the newness of my day, He's helping me to walk in my delieverane, he has blessed me with a blessing seen an unseen time after time.

To God be the glory for all the benefits he does on a daily basis nothing stays the same. It's time to reap what you have sown through the manifestation of God.

I Got a Testimony:

Who would have thought that a simple grain of salt and water would work wonders in your life?

I testified that I am a witness of its effects. I just recently experienced warm water with a mixture of salt to clear a sinus pressure headache that I've been dealing with for quite some time. A friend of mines been telling me to try this remedy for years just never took the time to do so. I bear witness today it works wonders I have no more pressure sinus headache, I've been healed and set free.

The cost of medication these days and the side effects is beyond discussion but the works of the Lord will live on forever. My God is a healer I can confess to that he delivered and healed me from sinus headaches pressure through salt and water up my nose. I speak life over any and every one that is experiencing these symptoms and I challenge you to try it.

Elijah heals Jericho's waters - II Kings 2:20-24; bring me a new jar and put salt in it, so they brought it to him. He went out to the spring of water and threw salt in it and said thus said the Lord. I have purified these waters there shall not be from there death or unfruitfulness any longer. So, the waters have been purified to this day according to the word of Elijah which he spoke ye are the salt of the earth.

Spiritual Nuggets: 2nd Timothy 2:15 study to show yourself approved Philippians 4:13-14; brethren I count not myself to have apprehended, but this one thing I do forgetting those things which are behind, and reaching forth unto those things which are before me, I press toward the mark for the prize of the High Calling of God in Christ Jesus.

Stay covered under the Blood of Jesus they cannot touch the blood in Jesus name. They may talk shop all day long but no weapon formed against thee shall prosper and every tongue that shall rise against thee in judgement I give you power to condemn it for that is the heritance of the servants of the Lord and their righteousness is of me says the Lord. That means I cover them and they are covered under my blood and I will dispatch ministering angels over you to protect you from all harm and danger. For you to live is Christ and for you to die is gain. I'm not speaking of a physical death says the Lord, I'm talking about an eternal prosperous gain in me.

Remember to stay prayerful: the enemy is listening to your thoughts to get you to have a spiritual abortion.

Glossary: satanic concentration; the total focus of satanic powers is upon individuals, organizations, governments, ministries; etc. Satan often focus on one person in which he can use at that time, rather it's in a church, family member, territory or a group of people to destroy, there's no exclusion of anyone.

Usually this person group or church have been called with a divine purpose that threatened Satan and his cohorts in which he seeks to abort their spiritual gains. Let's look over some of the territory he tried to invade, Joseph the nation of Israel, Esther Daniel's and Jesus.

Spiritual abortion is in the natural, so it is in the spirit the enemy seeks to apprehend and arrest the womb of the spirit in order to terminate that which is divine, so that his plans and purposes can be manifested. Thus, superimposing itself and over and over against the plans and purposes of God's people' Author Unknown.

So the beginning of every written word is to be search out every scripture you hear spoken over your life you should spend time to overlook it and ask God what it or they mean via its part of the spoken word or written word that is set before you as you study to show yourself approved a workman that needed not to be ashamed rightly dividing the word of truth that you may be understand and comprehend through research. To know God and his word for yourself on a daily basis concerning your life situation you going have to pick up your bible and search Him out for yourself.

As we continue, **I'll testify every time I get a chance**:

He forever watches over me and blesses me daily. He is our resource everything we need God supplies on a day to day basis, that he is always making a way out of no way. When I actually sit down and add up the cost on a weekly basic of my spending sometimes I have to shake my head and say thank you God in advance for increase.

I challenge you to just to take some time out of your busy schedule and count of the cost with your receipts of your spending on a day to day basic or weekly, whenever you spend your money. You will literally be surprise that God is forever supplying your needs with abundance of more than enough.

If it had not been for the Lord on my side and just for that I just want to say thank you.

So, the beginning of every written word spoken need to be search out through scripture, even if it's for how to pray, how to have faith, how to get your money out of the fishes' mouth. Whatever, your needs are go into the word of God and fine out where that scripture is and what it means to you ask God what you are saying to me.

Whatever word that is set before you even on this day study to show yourself approved a workman that needed not to be ashamed, but rightly dividing in the word of truth? That you may be established to know God's word for yourself concerning your life situation.

My Testimony II

You have been approved the fact that I got approved meant that I was not denied it has been delayed but it wasn't denied. This is when I came into the manifestation of the effectual fervent prayers of a righteous man availeth much my testimony of the manifestation of God's glory of the prophetic word that have been spoken over my life is came to pass. What I been praying for it might have been delayed, but it was not denied. I sought God out and asked him what that mean, do I need to go back and try it again. God said go and apply again. I'm a living testimony and I confess that God will approve you in the mists of your bad credit situation. I'm not saying that you shouldn't work on your credit because I had to clean up some things on my credit but it was not yet a 700-800 credit score either. But God, blessed me in the midst of my bad credit. I'm saying God will bless you when you in the progress when you show forth effort out of your obedience.

God eradicated the system and approved me for my car and it was the desire of my heart a Mercedes Benz something that I had desired long ago and he's getting ready to do greater. My property is coming regardless of the wait the foundation of the breakthrough is and will show up at the right time and that right soon.

Through the effectual fervent prayers of the righteous man that availeth much you can shout out God did it.

All the prayers that have been spoken over your life and throughout the churches at large. Repeat after me.

Be it unto me, and that right soon

Let it go and let God handle it

This battle is not yours to fight, the battle is the Lords

I trust you Lord, God you are my main resource

I believe you God, believe and you shall receive

God is able and he shall bring it to pass

Just shout thank you Jesus, three times and see wont he do it

To God be the Glory

Shout great grace to the mountain top

The peace of God that surpasses all your understanding

All these clichés and truism of certain words that went forth throughout every ministries that came forth out of the leaders mouth that spoke over your lives through prophetic prophecy, television, internet to encourage, uplift your spirit to trust in the Lord with all your heart and lean not to anyone else's understanding but seek God out for your directions and guidance.

The word of life that is written to guide your heart to know the spirit by the spirit. When you leave church, the conferences don't just walk out of there not knowing what to do until next Sunday come. You have to live this out throughout eternity. You have to walk in your delieverance. You have to walk my faith and not by what you hear or see. You have to make this your testimony and let it become your lifestyle.

For it is written; I came that you may have life and that more abundantly. Be not conformed to this world system. You are in this world but you are not of this world. Take authority over your mind. Know that you are not just shouting out the phrases or clichés that being spoken over your life in vain. Know that God is listening to your shout of praise. He inhabits the praises of his people. So when you hear these commandments go ahead and feel free to shout aloud and into the atmosphere let the devil hear you loud and clear. I will reap a harvest before this year end and forever more. I will trust in the Lord to open doors no man can close. I am that I Am, because God said I belong to him and no man can pluck me out of his hands.

Meditate and study on the word of God and believe God and stand firm on his words regardless of what the situation and circumstance is and that you find yourself in. Regardless of the problems you may be facing even in this day, regardless of the heavy weight of the bills that is overriding you right now. God is still able to bring you out just like he did for Shadrch, Meshach and Abednego they walked out of the fiery pit without being burned (caught up or left hanging without God's helping hand.) Just like he delivered Daniel out of the lions den, Daniel, shouted out my God is able to deliver:

God is able to deliver you forth from everything that you are wrestling with at this very moment. Seeking him in the name of Jesus know that, you know you're are not shouting those phrases in vain because God hears us and answers our cries unto him. Every word that is being spoken out of your mouth tonight and every cry you've cried throughout this year God's words are not going to return unto him void.

What God promised it will come to pass, you heard this song; it may not come when you want it but it will be there right on time. God is opening doors for you by this time tomorrow go and get what you've been asking God for and collect your goods don't stop at the door number one keep opening every door that is standing before you God has set you free to live out from the bondage of this world system.

Freedom from Bondage

To wake up from bondage and not be entangled with the cares of this world and live in other people matters and addictions Is like joy unspeakable joy.

Living a life of freedom almost seems unreal or impossible but, we know we serve a God that supplies all our needs according to His riches. That all things are possible though him when we cast all of our cares upon him take time out to remind him daily before your feet hit the floor for all He's doing for you on this day places you in a place to thank Him in advance for opening our eyes to see another day.

Learning to live again and be free from the entanglements of other people weights is the best thing you can encounter along with having more than enough to free yourself from lack. Lack of not having this, lack of not having that, lack of not being at peace, lack of not being joyful (happy.) just to name a few. Free yourself from the word lack.

lack: a state of being without having enough of something: absence, want, need, deficiency, insufficiency; deficit, unavailability, shortness, inadequacy, meagerness.

All the things that do not measure up to the provision that God has promised in our lives to have, "the Lord is my shepherd and I shall not want," is freedom. Freedom from things that come and attach itself to you to keep you living in poverty. There is no poverty in Christ, God owns the cattle on a thousand hills and he provides wisdom to get wealth. We come against the spirit of lack and poverty.

The anointing destroys the yoke because the oil flows freely to remove the weight of poverty and bondage off of your life. The oil provides coverage so the enemy can't grip you and keep you bond and enslaved you or keep your mind from thinking and speaking the word of truth over your life. It gives you a way of escape to help you slip away from the grip and onslaught of the devil. The oil brings back to your memory everything God has done for you in the pass and what He's doing for you even on this day.

As the oil flows from the top of your head to the depth of your soul it helps you to remember certain phrases in a song that brought you out of the some of the traps that had you bound: the devil thought he had me but God came and snatched me out of his hand. The anointing oil wouldn't let him hold you regardless of its grip, because the oil help set you free from the weight of the grip.

Freedom provides you a way of escape from the snares and cares of this world and every day you awaken to be free from the bondage of sin that tries to keep you bound where you can't speak to sickness and tell it you got to go. Once you experience freedom of bondage you can wake up with a new attitude.

The memory of the just is blessed remember back in the day when you grew up in the church, they had services for everything, the laying of hand, being anointed with oil like the oil that ran down Aaron's beard, take the oil home and anoint every room, your children, your job anoint every desk and chair before they get there, pour it in your husband shoes, your wives hair brush.

How many of you remember growing up in the church where they use to have services seven days of the week where the oil was apart of the service.

Growing Up in Church

Many times we may not have taken our testimony serious or even studying the word of God by memory or memorizing the names of the Bible, now that we have gotten older we get it, some people may be ashamed to get up and testify because of a lot of lack in their life, not living up to the total means of God's standards, now they have backslidden or don't go to church like they use to or ashamed that they need help or never received the word of God into their spirit or ever applied it to their lives or heart.

As adults some refuse to submit even at this time of their life because they still have that mindset nobody can tell them anything and the church lives inside of me and I don't need nobody teaching me nothing. That type of mentality can stop a lot of people from being under leadership. They won't be living large off of my money nor do some of them have a desire to learn again, but that's another subject or teaching at another time.

The major prophet was able to teach he minor prophets and the major prophets learn from the minor prophets saying that we can learn from each other just by the same way Zachariah and Haggai had the same message but received it differently but of the same time.

Get ready for the next chapter

Get ready to receive a greater move in the body of Christ, greater anointing greater blessings, greater works in a new time of refreshing is coming, recognizing the manifestation of God's breakthrough through prophetic prophecy and their different personalities is getting ready to overflow and drop in the churches at large and for the people.

Get ready for the manifestation of souls to run back into the Kingdom of God lay before him and repent of their sins for the time of refreshing has come. We are yet in the harvest season of sowing to reap what have already been sown. If you have been sowing seed over the last five to seven years get ready to receive your supernatural abundance of breakthroughs. The key word here is (already sown).

The song writer puts it this way (to reap what I have sown) therefore you have sown seed in the past along with what you have sown within this year of the last six months. Get ready and watch the move of God restoring, replenishing and returning income sown into the Kingdom of God. Your labor is not in vain you shall reap a harvest and I will compensate you out of your obedience and sacrifice. You sacrifice your income to bless those that spoke a word of life over your life with belief that God is able to deliver, God is able to heal, God is able to bring you out of that situation, God will supply all of your needs according to his riches and glory. Let the people of God shout "Glory" in this place.

Get ready to reap what you have sown in your past and yet even on this day it has not gone unnoticed. The enemy tried to blind your mind with doubt and fear that your breakthrough is not coming but; for it is written 1st Corinthians 2:9; eyes have not seen nor have ears heard nor have into entered into the heart of man the things which God has prepared for those that love him, move yourself out of the way and get in position and stay in position for within the next twenty-four hours (24) another transition of the power of the Holy Ghost is getting ready to release an anointing like never before and the reason I said never before is because everyday something new is happening in the atmosphere of the spirit realm. This is no time to get distracted turn off the television, stop eating everything in front of you, its time for fasting and praying, abstaining and consecrating yourself before God for this greater anointing that is getting ready to be released upon this land and in the Kingdom of God.

There is a greater remnant of leaders that have been holding back on the spirit of God and its time for them to spread the good news of what God is saying in the spirit realm. Through a new era of his anointing of the effectual fervent prayers of a righteous man that availeth much has taken a new position in the call of one's life. And, the manifestation of their prophetic breakthrough prayers that they have spoken is getting ready to come forth. Their time and labor have not been in vain. Every word that God has spoken is true nobodies mad but the devil. Now run and tell that.

Get ready for the mighty move of God, fresh wind has not stopped blowing, fresh fire has not stopped stirring, fresh anointing is still working through the laying on of hands and the oil being poured over their heads. Keep praying for breakthroughs in my people lives said the Lord. Don't give up Leaders; the people of God have been standing in the gap on your behalf as well. Your breakthroughs for your prayers are going to be manifested to. That change you have been praying for is coming to past and you shall reap your harvest in this season as well.

Prayer of Intercession

God gives us a heart to be on one accord and to know you in the parting of our sin know each other by our fruits. Give us a sure purpose for interceding on the behalf of each other's. Somewhere down the line we have slacked from remembering one of the commandments of praying on the behalf of our brother and sister. Continue to give us a heart to stay focused on prayer that we may comprehend the main focus that is hitting the mark in the areas in which we are called to pray.

We pray on the behalf of God's people concerning every circumstance and situation they are facing. Knowing that you hear and answer every petition of prayer request we lay before you and you immediately turn that situation around. And, for that God we thank you in advance for your power and grace that you have bestowed upon us.

As you destined intercessors that you have summoned to pray, we pray on the behalf of each family member that is present here to shift and transform them into a different level of position. We believe that God has changed some position for such a time as this. Thank you for the exaltation of the prayers that is going forth throughout this nation. Thank you for shifting and transforming the atmosphere in a new realm of intercession and breakthrough prayers.

CHAPTER TEN

Breakthrough Prayers

In closing having a pen as a ready writer, what's on your mind and what have you been thinking about lately, has been a very inspiring moment for me in these last few chapters. You will be amazed of what you actually can jot down through your thought pattern on a daily basis.

So many people are eager to here truth and testimony of others giving people hope to feel that they are not the only ones dealing with a certain matter and knowing what God has really done for you.

Sharing is caring about what you see others are actually dealing with on a day to day basis and just to share a few of your thoughts that you've been battling just similar situations and circumstances touches them and direct them to trust in the Lord concerning each and every situation they are dealing with on a different level is remarkable.

Here are some breakthrough prayers that the Holy Spirit have given me during my time of meditation an enlighten my heart and my mind today. Oh God, let your Glory train fill this temple as I touch and agree on the behalf of your nation and our people I pray for deliverance of breakthroughs over your peoples finances, marriages, husbands, wives and children their children children and the single parents mothers and fathers that you are restoring their home, bring them back together as one, supply all of their needs. Reestablish the love in their household O God meet the needs of the economical system over this nation O God provide educational funding's to help support the school system with the supplies for furthering their education for the teachers as well as the students.

I pray for salvation on the behalf of your people that are lost, set them apart from the cares of this world deliverance is for those that are battling addiction , deliverance is to bring them out of the things that have them bound with whatever addiction that is keeping them from living a holy and acceptable life before you and the Kingdom of God oh God all souls belong to you and they have been adopted into the body of Christ Ephesians 1:5 have it predestined unto the adoption of children by Jesus Christ to himself according to the good pleasure of his will.

Ezekiel 18:4 Behold all souls are mine says the Lord as the soul of the father so also the soul of the son is mine, the soul that sinneth, it shall not die let every man, woman, boy or girl take full responsibility over their own actions of their lives let no one hold the Kingdom of God or the leaders that are in the Kingdom of God responsible for how they should live outside your will in the body of Christ our Lord our Savior and Redeemer.

God, I thank you for touching the hearts of your people to call out the ones to intercede on behalf of others thank you in advance for the mighty move of God as you minister to each of us individually and collectively.

Thank you for your words of life as we search the scripture daily you said in them, we think we found life but its by your spirit we live move and have our being. Acts 17:28.

We are nothing without you our thoughts are not your thoughts and your ways are not our ways, you sit high and you look low and you know every hair upon our head God. You are the creator of all things Isaiah 55:8-9. Proverbs 15:3.

John 5:39: search the scriptures for in them we think we have eternal life and they are they which testify of me.

Acts 17:11: these were the noble than those in Thessalonica in that they received the word with all readiness of mind and search the scripture daily whether those things were so.

As we continue to pray on the behalf of the world, as I continue to pray on the behalf of the world, the nation, the city and states and for your people. We ask you to put a hedge of protection around this world and each one of us.

Let us decrease as you increase in each and every one of their hearts as they lay aside everyone of their cares and concerns for the time of intercession and on the behalf of others.

God you are the mediator that stands in the gap for every prayer that has been prayed over your people's life. God, I know your main concern is for your people and for that I say thank you in advance for all of your mighty acts that you have performed in their lives, God how you have healed their love ones, bless their marriages to stay together, provided jobs for those that were jobless, how you have sent forth breakthroughs after breakthroughs. Open doors when some doors were impossible to open. Closed doors when the enemy came to steal, kill and destroy their children. You stepped in God and you said you never seen the righteous forsaken nor your seed begging for bread. You pulled down strongholds that were seen and unseen attacks when the works of darkness stood behind our backs and threw fiery darts like a wicked man that did not care.

Father God for that I say thank you in Jesus name and it is so.

James 5:16: confess your faults one to another and pray for one another that you may be healed the effectual fervent prayer of a righteous man availeth much.

Job 1:10 hast not thou made a hedge about him about his house and about all that he hath on every side? Thou have blessed the work of his hands, and his substance is increased in the land.

As I conclude, Father God, concerning having a pen as a ready writer and the things that has been on my mind and what I've been thinking lately, I pray you send forth a fire anointing to each hand that touch the pages of this book. Allow them to receive a revelation from You concerning their needs and desire in becoming an author. Let them find honest and willing publishers that would be patient and understanding for their first novel as you have given me. I release a magnetic breakthrough of blessing to everyone from this time forward. In Jesus' name.

Thank you, in advance, for supernatural breakthroughs over our healing from all our soul diseases. Thank you for supernatural breakthroughs over our finances in the birthing of our new businesses. Thank you for a supernatural unification in the body of Christ and the churches at large.

I pray and I know that you are able to do exceedingly and abundantly above all we can ask or think for the good of them that love you, to them who are called according to your will and purposes. Roman 8:28

Father God you give us the power to speak healing over our lives. Through your words that says in Luke 10:19; Behold, I give you power of treading upon serpents and scorpions and over all the power of the enemy, and nothing shall in anywise injure you. Are you hearing that people of God? Nothing shall in anywise injure you. Although it is formed against you, it shall not harm you.

The enemy has injured a lot of God's people by taking them out of here through premature death for those that remain saideth the Lord "no weapon formed against you shall prosper; from this day forward shall prosper or injure you." Isaiah 54:17.

My prayer is that you share the word with power to overcome the snares and attacks that the enemy has released upon you, your family and the people of God and all (those that are called by his name) so, that they can be prepared when the devil releases an attack they can come back in the name of Jess and release a counter attack upon the works of his imps and return them back unto him with their works undone. Psalms 70. Speak the word.

Thank you for all your wisdom, knowledge and understanding over every work of darkness that comes to distract the power of your healings, deliverance and breaksthroughs over your people.

The blood of Jesus is there to shield and protect you from all harm and danger, for when I see the blood posted on the door in Exodus 12:33; he will not allow the destroyer to enter your houses and strike you down. And I declare that "no weapon formed against them shall prosper, no illnesses that your people are wrestling with even on this day should override and take any more of them out of here in Jesus' name.

I cast down vain imagination of thoughts and report of any negative disease that was given by their family members, their peers, their loved ones and the doctors report, I decree and declare that the people of God during this new wave moment to start speaking over their lives I will believe the report of the Lord and his report will cleanse me and your people. They are healed delivered and set free from all soul diseases that was ever spoken over our lives in Jesus' name we pray.

I take authority over every negative thought given against your word that give your people life more abundantly I decree and declare the words of the living that has all power to rule over all things that speak a word of truth that the divine wisdom of your divine power of your wisdom knowledge and understanding over every foul demonic force of evil and speak life to the lame and they shall walk, we operate out of your power with a high revolution of power and spit on the blind eyes and they shall recover their sight God we speak forth with power and authority that you have given to us with the gift of the Holy Ghost.

For it is written, "Thou also shall decree a thing and it shall be established unto thee; and the light shine upon thy ways" Job 22:28.

Thank you, Father, in advance for my prayers and supplication with thanksgiving I pray our requests be made known unto you O God, which surpasses all our understanding in Christ Jesus I pray.

(Philippians 4:6-7). I also pray for your will to be done over your people throughout the world.

Father God, as I close this prayer on the behalf of your people, I thank you once again in advance for answering my prayers as I laid aside my thoughts, desires and needs to intercede on behalf of others. I petition silently before your throne of mercy and grace and the throne room of your heart.

I declared that the effectual fervent prayer of a righteous man availeth much and that your will be done concerning your people. Let it be done concerning their will and according to their faith and from this day forward that they may tear down and cast out every sickness or disease that has attached itself to their body mind and soul on this day. God, you said that you're always praying on our behalf to your Father which art in heaven and you are forever interceding on our behalf so, I touch and agree with their will that with your stripes they are healed delivered and set free from the cares of this world. I pray that they be free from every jezebel spirit that carry the form of witchcraft and lying.

For it is written, "They should decree a thing and it shall be established your word". Whose report will you believe? I will believe the report of the Lord; I am healed, delivered, and set free from all of my soul diseases.

Now, start thanking Him in advance for the victory already won and for being a mediator over your prayers and start acknowledging Him as being Lord over your life.

God will acknowledge your prayers and petitions unto himself because he is the Father, the Son and the Holy Ghost and he stands firm at his promises. He cares for you; He promised to never leave nor forsake you. In the hours of your prayers, lay before him. Amen, and it is so.

THE END

All of this came into fruition by having a ready pen by the bedside. Having a pen as a ready writer just went off as a light bulb and I started writing to conquer those thoughts that was going on in my mind and all of those other things that I have been wanting to jot down and formed them inside a book, all the things that I have been thinking about lately and wanting to share part of my life experiences and my divine interventions. My journey is not over and there's more to share, who knows could there be a second volume of "Having a pen as a ready writer.

Please note the difference so that you may continue to study the scripture to show yourself approved of what you heard, read and what's being spoken over your life. Psalms 45:1; in what is actually being stated in this word. Below is a few of them that drew me near when I read it for myself. KJV:" My heart is indicting a good matter: I speak of the things which I have made touching the King: my tongue is "the pen of a ready writer." spoken of over your life.

I fell in love with this one. TLB:" My heart is "overflowing with beautiful thoughts:" I will write a lovely poem to the King; for I am as "full of words" as the speediest writer pouring out his (mine) story. Enjoy the journey..........

www.ingramcontent.com/pod-product-compliance
Lightning Source LLC
LaVergne TN
LVHW051644080426
835511LV00016B/2490